Happiness Every Day for Kids

written by
Safiya Hussain

illustrations by
Jameelah Munshi | Blesink

New Age Publishers UK

HAPPINESS EVERY DAY for *KIDS*
Copyright © Safiya Hussain 2021

All Rights Reserved

Safiya Hussain has asserted her rights under the Copyright, Designs and Patents Act 1988 and/or international copyright law to be identified as the author of this work.

This book is sold subject to the condition that it shall not, by way of trade or otherwise, be lent, resold, hired out, or otherwise circulated without the publisher's and author's consent and without a similar condition, including this condition, being imposed on the subsequent purchaser.

Published by New Age Publishers UK, 4th Floor, Media Factory, Kirkham Street, Preston, England, PR1 2HE.

ISBN 978-0-9931895-2-4

Happiness Every Day for Kids

Books also by Safiya Hussain:
Three Thousand Miles for a Wish
Happiness Every Day (adults)

Foreword

The facts in this book are stated to the best of my knowledge. I do not claim to be an Islamic Scholar or anything else of the sort, and so, if I have made any errors or caused any offence, I apologise in advance and hope to be pardoned.

I have made reference to Prophet Mohammad (pbuh) but have chosen to omit the words 'peace be upon him', which usually follow afterwards, for the readers ease and to preserve the flow of the book. Please include these words when reading if you wish to do so.

Also, please note that all the quotes of Prophet Muhammad (pbuh) are from authentic hadiths but have not been referenced to also preserve the flow of the book.

In the name of Allah, the Most Merciful, the Most Beneficent

For my children, and for you too

Just a Note

The moment you opened your eyes when you were born, your chase for happiness began. Your soul began searching for comfort, purpose, peace and joy.

It is not just you looking for happiness. People before you, and people after you, all over the world, had, and will have, the same want to just be happy.

Perfect and Forever Happiness

Before I talk to you about happiness in every day, I want to first talk to you about perfect and forever happiness.

Perfect and forever happiness exist. No fights, no hatred, no jealousy, no sadness and no death. That pure, perfect everlasting joy is out there.

But not in this world.

Perfect and forever happiness is saved for the after-life, beyond the skies, in Heaven.

Why? Because God, Allah, did not plan for Heaven to be on Earth. Life on this planet is a test of your love for Allah. Through the happiness and sadness He puts in your life, how faithful and loving do you remain to Allah?

The sooner you realise that perfect happiness does not exist in this world and that there will always be a mixture of happiness and sadness in your life, then the sooner you will be on your way to becoming happier every day.

Happiness Every Day

Even in the hard times in your life, moments of happiness can easily be found every day. They will not be forever lasting moments, as that is life, but they are moments that will boost your day.

Happiness mainly depends on how positively you think and act. It does not so much matter how much money you have, where you live or what you look like.

This book will help you change the way you think and act, day by day, so you become happier in life.

How to Use the Book

This book is very easy to use.

- Start on Day 1 and follow the steps
- If you cannot do a certain task, then pick another random day
- Once the year is over, well done! And let's start again.

Finally, I pray. I pray that you find happiness every day, from today onwards. And I pray that you will one day find forever happiness, in Allah's Heaven. Ameen.

Day 1
Ask Allah for happiness

What to do
Raise your hands, close your eyes and say "Allah, please make me happy".

Why?
Allah is the Giver and Taker of happiness. If you ask Him for happiness, then He will give it to you in some way or another. Du'aa (asking Allah) is your strongest power in the world.

Allah...
Allah says in the Quran *'...indeed I am near. I answer the prayer of every caller (silent or audible) when he calls upon Me ...'* - 2:186.

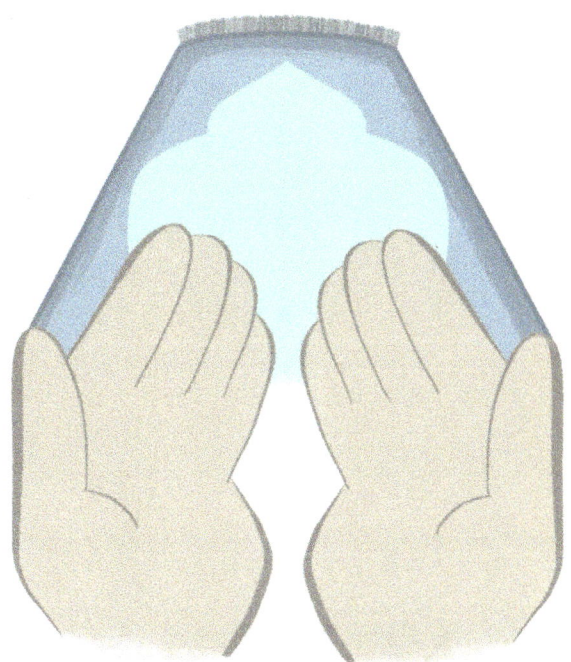

Day 2
Imagine heaven

What to do

Close your eyes and imagine being in Heaven. Imagine flying through skies, drinking from chocolate fountains, having every single toy in the world. What else would you wish for? Ask Allah to give you Heaven one day, and *insha'Allah* (Allah willing) He will.

Why?

Smile, be excited and look forward to Heaven.

Allah...

Prophet Muhammad (pbuh) said; 'Allah says: "I have prepared for My righteous slaves that which no eye has seen, no ear has heard and it has never crossed the mind of man"'.

Day 3
Go outdoors

What to do

Go out somewhere nice, like the park, beach or riverside. Run, walk, skip. Breathe in the fresh air, feel the wind on your face, and hear the birds.

Why?

Fresh air and daylight will refresh your mind and body, and make you feel happier.

Allah...

Notice the amazing world Allah has created *'...And they think deeply about the creation of the Heavens and the Earth, [saying] "Our Lord! You did not create (all) of this without a purpose, glory be to You"...'* - Quran 3:191.

Day 4
Turn your day into worship

What to do

When doing anything today, do it to please Allah. Smile, be kind, be thankful for your food, say your prayers, talk to Allah about your wants, sleep well, don't argue - Allah loves all these good things.

Why?

You were born to only please and worship Allah. And so doing the things you were born to do will make you happy and peaceful.

Allah...

Allah says *'I have not created jinn and mankind (for any purpose) except to worship Me'* - Quran 51:56.

Day 5
Note a positive moment

What to do

Write down one positive thing that has happened to you in the last day. It might be the fun you had in the garden; did you look for worms? Was it sunny? Did you have an ice lolly? Read the note throughout the day.

Why?

When you write about good things, and keep reading them, your mind relives the good times and this will make you feel happy again.

Allah...

Thank Allah for this moment. He says '...*if you are grateful, I will certainly grant you more [favours]...*' - Quran 14:7.

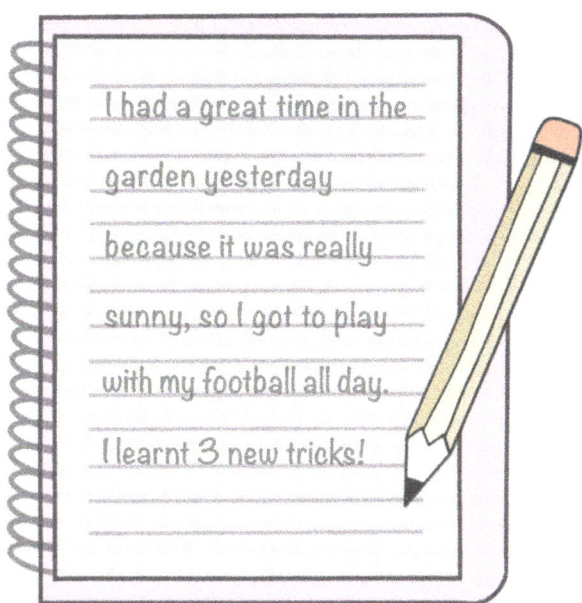

Day 6
Sleep well

What to do
Have a good nights sleep tonight. Turn off your gadgets, put your toys away, hug your pillow, and close your eyes.

Why?
Sleep is very important for your mind and body to feel happy and energised the next day. It is worth more than $60,000 a year!

Allah...
Sleep is a great gift from Allah. *'And remember when He made slumber fall upon you as a means of serenity from Him'* - Quran 8:11.

Day 7
Give someone a flower

What to do
Go to your garden or the park and pick out a flower. Give it to someone, like your mother, father or brother.

Why?
This is a sweet gesture of love to the lucky person, and when they smile, it will make you smile too.

Allah...
This will also please Allah which will get you rewards; *'Is there any reward for good, other than good?'* - Quran 55:60.

Day 8
Notice Allah's signs

What to do
Notice everything you see, feel, hear, touch and smell all day. These are signs of Allah – your jam toast, the wind on your face, your mother's gentle touch.

Why?
Seeing Allah's signs will show you how kind, great and amazing He is. For this, you will love Him, worship Him and feel happy that He is everywhere around you.

Allah...
Allah says; *'Verily! In the creation of the Heavens and the Earth, and in the alternation of night and day, there are indeed signs for those who have intelligence'* - Quran 3:190.

Day 9
Exercise

What to do
Do some exercise today. Get up and go run in the garden, skip in your bedroom, or do some sit-ups.

Why?
Scientists say that exercise is very important for happiness as when you exercise, chemicals are sent to your brain that make you feel happy. Exercise also makes you healthier, look trimmer, think better and sleep well.

Allah...
Thank Allah for gifting you a healthy body to exercise; *'Then which of your Lord's favours will you deny?'* - Quran 55:13.

Day 10
You are richer than billions

What to do
You are richer more than the billions of children that have come on Earth. Look around you and spot all the luxuries that were not around hundreds of years ago, even for princes and princesses. Like; hot water, TV, scooters, the internet, schools.

Why?
Knowing how rich you are today compared to other children will make you be thankful and happy.

Allah...
Say *Alhamdulillah* (all praise and thanks is to Allah) for all these luxuries. Allah says; *'So take what I have given you and be of the grateful ones'* - Quran 7:144.

Day 11
Smile lots

What to do
Smile lots today, even if you don't feel like smiling.

Why?
When you smile, positive signals and thoughts are sent to your brain that then make you feel happy. Smiling at other people will also make them happy.

Allah...
Smiling pleases Allah too and will gain you reward; *'to smile in the face of your brother is charity given on your behalf'* - Prophet Muhammad (pbuh).

Day 12
Write all you're grateful for

What to do
Write down all the things you are grateful for. This could be; the love of your mother, your clothes, your strong legs to walk.

Why?
When you are grateful you will be happier.

Allah...
Also, thank Allah for all these things He has given you – He will be pleased with you and give you even more. '...*If you are grateful, I will certainly grant you more [favours]...*' - Quran 14:7.

Day 13
Control your state of mind

What to do

Keep your mind calm no matter what is happening around you - even if it's raining outside, your brother is arguing or you've lost your bag. Think happy thoughts, take away sad thoughts and remember that life is about pleasing Allah.

Why?

Life on the outside can't always be controlled by you, but if you keep your mind inside positive then you will feel happy.

Allah...

Remember your purpose, as Allah says; *'I have not created jinn and mankind (for any purpose) except to worship Me'* - Quran 51:56.

Day 14
You have the world

What to do
Look around you; are you safe, healthy, and have enough food for the day?

Why?
If the answer is yes, then smile, because you have the world.

Allah...
Prophet Muhammed (pbuh) said *'He, upon whom morning comes while being safe and sound, healthy in his body, and having the sustenance of his day, seems as if the entire world has been granted for him'*.

Day 15
Give to the needy

What to do

Give something away to the needy – perhaps one of your toys to the charity shop, some food to your old neighbour or some money from your savings box to an orphanage.

Why?

Scientists say that when you give to people who need your help, you will feel happier.

Allah...

When you give to the needy, Allah is also very pleased and you will be rewarded; *'whatever good you spend, He will replace it [with better]....'* - Quran 34:39.

Day 16
Don't worry about money

What to do

Don't worry about money, and having nice things. Allah set the amount of wealth you will get in your life, before you were born. Nothing you do will change it. But ask Allah to put blessings in what you have so even a little can go a long way.

Why?

So stop worrying about and chasing money or expensive things, and you'll feel happier.

Allah...

Prophet muhammad (pbuh) said *'If the son of Adam ran away from his provision as he runs away from death, then his provision would find him just as death finds him.'*

Day 17
Trust Allah like the bird does

What to do
Trust Allah today, like the birds trust Allah. A bird flies out in the morning hungry and comes back full. Say 'I trust you Allah' and believe He will look after you like He looks after the birds.

Why?
By trusting Allah to take care of you, you will feel happy.

Allah...
Prophet Muhammed (pbuh) said. *'If you were to rely upon Allah with the reliance He is due, you would be given provision like the birds: They go out hungry in the morning and come back with full bellies in the evening'.*

Day 18
Sadness is a blessing

What to do

If you are feeling sad, remember that sadness is a blessing. Allah makes you sad sometimes so that you will make du'aa, remember that you're here to worship Allah, and to be patient - which will all earn you Heaven.

Why?

Be happy that your sadness reminds you of Allah and will mean you will get Heaven.

Allah...

'...But give good news to those who patiently persevere' - Quran 2:155.

Day 19
Note 3 things you're grateful for

What to do
Write down all the things you are grateful for. This could be your good eyesight, the delicious sandwich you ate earlier, your comfy bed.

Why?
When you are grateful for what you have, you will be happier.

Allah...
Also, thank Allah for all these things He has given you – He will be pleased with you and give you even more. *'...If you are grateful, I will certainly grant you more [favours]...'* - Quran 14:7.

Day 20

Learn about stars

What to do

Learn about stars. How do stars differ? How many are there? How long do they exist for? What are they made up of? What benefit do they give you?

Why?

Learning something new and interesting will stop you from getting bored, amaze your mind and make you feel happy.

Allah...

'And He has placed the night and the day at your service, the sun and the moon; and the stars are also kept in servitude by His Command. Surely, in this are proofs for people of understanding' - Quran 16:12.

Day 21
Gratefulness and patience

What to do

For good things you have, show thanks and love to your Lord, who gave it. He will be pleased. For sad things, show patience by trusting your Lord and still showing Him love. He will be pleased.

Why?

When Allah is pleased with you, He will give you Heaven *insha'Allah*. This will make you happy.

Allah...

Allah says; *'I have rewarded them this day for their patience and faithfulness: they are indeed the ones that have achieved bliss...'* - Quran 23:111.

Day 22
Ask Allah for Heaven

What to do

Write down 5 things that you dream to have. Do you want; a magic carpet? Endless ice cream? To meet Allah? Ask Allah for it and truly believe you will have them in Heaven.

Why?

Heaven is real, and one day you will have all these things plus more! Smile and look forward to it.

Allah...

Allah says '... *In Heaven, there will be whatever the heart desires, whatever pleases the eye ....*' - Quran 43:71.

Day 23
Link your heart to Allah

What to do

Keep your link close to Allah the most. Focus on Allah, His love, and doing things that please Him. Don't think too much about yourself, your toys, and even people around you. You came from Allah and you will go back to Him. He is your creator, always by your side, will never leave you. Allah is your world and more.

Why?

Keeping linked to Allah will give you peace and happiness, and open Heaven's doors for you.

Allah...

'...to Allah we belong and to Him we shall return' - Quran 2:156.

Day 24
Success is good deeds

What to do

Ask yourself; 'am I successful?' but not in the sense of money, beauty or popularity. In the sense of your good deeds. How kind are you? How much do you thank Allah? Is Allah pleased with you?

Why?

It only matters what Allah thinks of you, and He only cares about your good deeds. Don't worry about anything else. If you are successful with Allah, then Heaven will be your prize.

Allah...

'As for those whose scale (of good deeds) are heavy, they will be the successful ones (by entering Paradise)' - Quran 7:8.

Day 25
Watch the sunrise

What to do
Wake up early to watch the sunrise – from your bedroom window or from your back yard. The sunrise is one of the greatest natural scenes that Allah blesses us with every day. A magical gift that brings our world out of the darkness and cold, and into the light and warmth – much like life's story of sadness and happiness.

Why?
To pause, watch the sunrise and think about life will give you a great start to your day.

Allah...
'It is He who made the sun a shining light...' - Quran 10:5.

Day 26
Meet a good friend

What to do

Meet or call a good friend. A good friend is a good person, who is positive, doesn't complain and argue, and shows happiness.

Why?

Friendship with good people is one of life's greatest joys, as their good vibes will spread to you.

Allah...

Prophet Muhammad's (pbuh) advice is that friend's vibes spread and so to keep friends *'whose appearance reminds you of God, and whose speech increases you in knowledge, and whose actions remind you of the Hereafter'*.

Day 27
Accept Allah's decisions

What to do

Accept all that Allah has decided for you. Whether you've got a bike or you haven't. Whether you are super clever or not. Allah is the most-wise, makes the best decisions and He knows what is good for you. So be grateful, be patient and trust Allah to be doing what is best for you.

Why?

Accepting Allah's decisions about your life will make you feel happy.

Allah..

This will also please Allah. *'...And it may be that you dislike a thing which is good for you and that you like a thing which is bad for you. Allah knows but you do not know'* - Quran 2:216.

Day 28
Practice gratitude and patience

What to do

Look in the mirror and say: "today, for good things, I promise to be grateful by saying 'thank you Allah', and showing Him love. And, for bad things, I promise to be patient, trust Allah and still show Him love"

Why?

By being grateful you will feel happier. By being patient you will feel peace.

Allah...

Allah will reward you for being grateful and patient. *'...If you are grateful, I will certainly grant you more [favours]...'* - Quran 14:7. *'I have rewarded them this day for their patience and faithfulness...'* - Quran 23:111.

Day 29
Plan a trip to a museum

What to do
Plan a visit to a museum soon. Or if you can't go, take your mind back to 6,000 years ago. Look around and think what would have been different for you. Where would you live? What would you eat? What would you play with?

Why?
This will fascinate you and also make you feel happy to live in modern times.

Allah...
Alhamdulillah. 'And if you were to count the blessings of Allah, never will you be able to count them' - Quran 14:34.

Day 30
Act how you want to feel

What to do
If you want to feel happy today then first you must act happy. Be positive, jokey, smiley and energetic.

Why?
When you act happy, real feelings of happiness will soon follow.

Allah...
Ask Allah to make you feel happy too; *'Call upon Me; I will respond to you'* - Quran 40:60.

Day 31
Your heart is a ticking timer

What to do

Feel your heart beat. Tick tock tick tock. It is like a ticking timer. The alarm has been set for when it is time for you to go back to Allah. As your heart ticks, use every second to please Allah - remember Him, pray, be nice, smile, be thankful, don't argue.

Why?

Be happy knowing that you will meet Allah and His Heaven.

Allah...

'The one who remembers death most often and the one who is well-prepared to meet it; these are the wise; honorable in this life and dignified in the Hereafter' - Prophet Muhammad (pbuh).

Day 32
Drink plenty of water

What to do

Carry a water bottle with you everywhere, and drink lots of water (1.5 litres). Did you know your body is made of 80% water?

Why?

When you drink enough water it boosts your energy, improves happiness, flushes out toxins, helps you think better and makes you look fresher.

Allah...

Thank Allah for this great blessing and know that He; *'... created every living thing from water'* - Quran 21:30.

Day 33
Love Allah the most

What to do
Who or what do you love the most? Your mother, father, toys, bike, games console? Whatever it is, change it to 'I love Allah the most'. *'Laa illaha illallah'* means, 'there is no diety worthy of worship except Allah'. You were born to love Allah the most.

Why?
Your heart, body and soul belong with Allah and so will be happiest when you love Allah the most.

Allah..
'...*Those that truly believe, love Allah more than anything else...*' - Quran 2:165.

Day 34
Go for a walk outside

What to do
Get some fresh air and go for a 30 minute walk outside in the daylight. Even if it's raining, snowing or windy.

Why?
Walking, especially in the daylight, makes your body relax, keeps it healthy, clears your mind and boosts your happiness.

Allah...
Whilst you're out, marvel at the world Allah has created. '..."Our Lord! You did not create (all) of this without a purpose, glory be to You"...' - Quran 3:191.

Day 35
Wear something nice

What to do
Wear something nice today; a bright coloured top, a pretty dress, a twinkling bracelet?

Why?
The most important time of your life is right now, as the past has gone and the future may never come. Today is special, so dress special to feel special.

Allah...
Also, Allah will be pleased if you are clean, neat and well-dressed. *'Allah is beautiful and likes beauty'* - Prophet Muhammad (pbuh).

Day 36
Worries will be forgotten

What to do
List 5 worries you've had in the past. Maybe it was on your first day at school or when sitting on a roller coaster? See how Allah helped you through and you are not worried anymore?

Why?
Allah will also help you with current worries, and soon they will be forgotten too, *insha'Allah* (Allah willing). Remember this and smile.

Allah...
Allah tells us life on Earth will be soon forgotten. *'This worldly life is a trivial [fleeting] gain. Undoubtedly, the Hereafter, is really a place to live'* - Quran 40:39.

Day 37
Do something nice for parents

What to do
Do something nice for your mother, father or carer. Make them breakfast, help them with the cleaning, tell them a funny story.

Why?
When you do nice things for people, they will feel happy and you will feel happy.

Allah...
Also, Allah will be happy with you as He says you should honor your parents, speak with them respectfully, *'lower to them the wing of humility, and say: "My Lord! Show them Mercy as they raised me when I was young"'* - Quran 17:24.

Day 38
Everything is borrowed

What to do

Everything you have in your life is not yours, but is a loaned gift from Allah. Your mother, your brother, your cute cat, your toys, your hands; all of it is a loaned gift from Allah and is not yours to keep forever. Each gift will one day be taken back by Allah.

Why?

Knowing everything is borrowed will make you thankful, and help you make the most of what you have with happiness.

Allah...

'Surely, to Allah we belong, and to Him we shall return' - Quran 2:156.

Day 39

Note a positive moment

What to do

Write down one positive thing that has happened to you in the last day. It might be when your uncle took you for ice cream? Where did you go? Did you have sprinkles? Read the note throughout the day.

Why?

When you write about good things, and keep reading them, your mind relives the good times and this will make you feel happy again.

Allah...

Thank Allah for this moment. He says *'...if you are grateful, I will certainly grant you more [favours]...'* - Quran 14:7.

Positive Moment of the Day

Day 40
Be patient with sadness

What to do

What's been making you sad? Close your eyes and say to Allah; 'Allah, please do what is best for me. I will be patient, I will trust You, and I will still love You'.

Why?

When you are patient (are not too sad and complain) and trust Allah to take care of everything, then you will feel good.

Allah...

Allah will love you for being patient and promises Heaven; *'I have rewarded them this day for their patience and faithfulness: they are indeed the ones that have achieved bliss...'* - Quran 23:111.

Day 41
Remember life's purpose

What to do

Spend two minutes – in the morning, afternoon and evening – to stop, close your eyes, and remember your life's purpose. 'I am here to please Allah'. So act on it; be nice to others, pray, be thankful, don't complain, remember Allah.

Why?

Doing what you were born to do will make you feel happy. It will also please Allah and earn you Heaven.

Allah...

'I have not created jinn and mankind (for any purpose) except to worship Me' - Quran 51:56.

Day 42
No one owes you anything

What to do

Realise that no one owes you anything, and any good that someone does for you is a bonus. Your friend doesn't have to always play with you, or your brother doesn't have to share his sweets with you (unless mum says!). Everyone has a free choice and you can't force them.

Why?

Be happy when someone is kind to you as it's a bonus, but don't be sad if they are not.

Allah...

Thank Allah for the bonuses, as He says; *'...If you are grateful, I will certainly grant you more [favours]...'* - Quran 14:7.

Day 43
10 things you're grateful for

What to do

In your day, write 10 things that you are thankful for. This could be; your soft pillow, your blue toothbrush, playing with your friend, your kind mother, your jam sandwich. Smile and say *alhamdulillah* for each thing.

Why?

When you are grateful you will be happier.

Allah...

In Islam, half of happiness is to be grateful, and is pleasing to Allah. *'Therefore remember Me. I will remember you. And be grateful to Me and do not be ungrateful'* - Quran 2:152.

Day 44
Light a candle

What to do

Ask an adult to light a candle in the evening; when you have dinner or when making your prayers.

Why?

Watching a candle's flame is very soothing and will make you feel happy.

Allah...

Thank Allah for the gift of candles. *'And He has made everything in the Heavens and Earth of service to you. It is all from Him. These are certainly signs [of Allah's powers] for people who reflect'* - Quran 45:13.

Day 45
Eat healthily

What to do

Eat 5 pieces of fruit or vegetables today. Blend them to make a smoothie, make a juice, have a fruit salad lunch. Maybe take vitamins too.

Why?

Scientists say that eating healthily improves your happiness.

Allah...

Respecting your body with healthy food also pleases Allah; *'O mankind, Eat of what is lawful and wholesome on the Earth...'* - Quran 2:168.

Day 46
Speak of positive moments

What to do
Tell someone about 3 positive things that have happened today. Maybe you found an acorn, met an old cousin, had a delicious burger.

Why?
When sharing good times, you relive the moments and feel the happiness again.

Allah...
Thank Allah too as it pleases Him; *'Therefore remember Me. I will remember you. And be grateful to Me and do not be ungrateful'* - Quran 2:152.

Day 47
Turn off electronic devices

What to do
For a couple of hours, turn off all electronic devices – phone, computer, T.V. Do something of quality; play a board game with your family, have a chat with your sister, read a good book, try making something.

Why?
Electronic devices waste time, affect sleep and increase sadness.

Allah...
Thank Allah for the simple and natural gifts He has given you. *Alhamdulillah* (all praise and thanks be to Allah).

Day 48
Live like it's your last day

What to do

Live today as though it's your last day. That doesn't mean you should be sad, but to do things that you have been put on earth for - to worship Allah. So do things that please Allah; go to school and learn, be kind, say your prayers, be thankful for food, make du'aa for what you want, trust Allah.

Why?

If it is your last day, then you will not have wasted it. This will make you feel happy.

Allah...

'I have not created jinn and mankind (for any purpose) except to worship Me' - Quran 51:56.

Day 49
Don't speak bad of anyone

What to do

Promise not to say a bad word about anyone today. Even if a boy pushes past you in school, or if your little sister eats your last sweet. Say something good instead, or say nothing.

Why?

Saying bad words will make your soul sad.

Allah...

And saying bad words will also displease Allah *'Never spy and never backbite one another...'* - Quran 49:12.

Day 50
Give extra toys to charity

What to do

Empty your drawers of toys you've not played with for a year. Give them to a charity.

Why?

Having too many things will give you stress. Living simply and also giving to the poor, will make you feel happy.

Allah...

Allah will be pleased with you. Prophet Muhammad (pbuh) said: *'the son of Adam will not pass away from Allah until he is asked about five things...'*, the fourth being; *'how did he spend his wealth...'*

Day 51
Please Allah

What to do

Please Allah all day today - say your prayers, do nice things to others, don't argue, thank Allah for what He's given you, trust Allah to be by your side.

Why?

You were born to please Allah, and so nothing can make you happier than doing what you were born to do.

Allah..

Allah says that He promises; *'gardens under which rivers flow, where they shall live forever, and beautiful mansions in Eternal Heaven. But the greatest bliss (happiness) is the Good Pleasure of Allah. That is the ultimate success.'* - Quran 9:72.

Day 52
Be like a traveller

What to do
Imagine you are on a train; you sit, snack, talk, play but always waiting for your destination. Life is like being on a train called Earth. You are on Earth but should be waiting for your final destination, which is Heaven. Always remember this.

Why?
You will feel happy that Earth is just a temporary journey and that you have an exciting final destination to get to.

Allah...
Prophet Muhammad advised; *'be in this world as though you are a traveller'*.

Day 53
Spend time with someone

What to do

Spend an hour with someone you love. Maybe help your mother cook? Play a game with your little brother? Have a chat with your father? Enjoy the company.

Why?

Allah made you in such a way that you have a natural human need to be close with others. So this will make you happy.

Allah...

'And Allah has made for you from your homes a place of rest' - Quran 16:80.

Day 54
Ask Allah for what you want

What to do

Ask Allah for what you want. Do you want good grades? More friends? Allah is the Giver and Taker of everything. If you ask Him for something, then He will give it to you in some way. Du'aa (asking Allah) is your strongest power in the world.

Why?

Be happy knowing you have this special power called 'du'aa'.

Allah...

Making du'aa pleases Allah too; '...indeed I am near. I answer the prayer of every caller (silent or audible) when he calls upon Me ...' - Quran 2:186. 'when He wills anything, His only command is to say "Be!" – and it is'- Quran 36:82

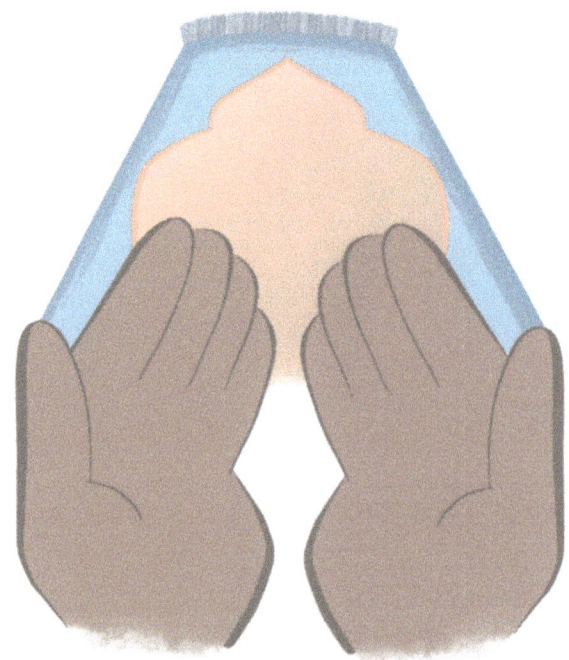

Day 55
Write 'A' for Alhamdulillah

What to do

Write an 'A' on the back of your hand. 'A' for *Alhamdulillah* (all praise and thanks be to Allah). Every time you see that A, look around you for something that Allah has gifted you with; a sunny day, a drink, chocolate, a seat on the bus? Each time, smile and say *alhamdulillah*.

Why?

When you are grateful for what you have, you will be happier.

Allah...

Allah will be very pleased with you if you are grateful. *'...And Allah will soon reward the grateful ones'* - Quran 3:144.

Day 56
Exercise

What to do
Do some exercise. Do 100 star jumps, 50 runs up and down the stairs, and then 100 star jumps again..

Why?
Scientists say that exercise is very important for happiness, as happy chemicals are released after exercise into your brain. Also, people who exercise are healthier, look trimmer, think more clearly and sleep better.

Allah...
Prophet Muhammad (pbuh) advises you to look after your body, which is a gift from Allah by exercising. *'Then which of your Lord's favours will you deny?'* - Quran 55:13.

Day 57
Act and speak positive

What to do
Speak positive words and act positive. Smile, say you feel good, act cheerful and don't complain.

Why?
If you act negatively, you will feel more sad, but if you act and speak positively then you will feel happier.

Allah...
'Blessed is the man who speaks good and is triumphant; or keeps silent in the face of evil and is secure' - Prophet Muhammad (pbuh).

Day 58
Be happy for others

What to do

When you see someone looking happy, riding a nice bike, going on holiday, eating a big bag of sweets, smile and try to be happy for them. Allah has decided to give some people more, and some people less and He is the best decider. Accept it, be happy with it.

Why?

When you do not feel jealous, your heart will feel pure, free and happy.

Allah...

Allah will be pleased with you for being happy with others. *'He is not a true believer, until he wants for his brother, what he wants for himself'* - Prophet Muhammad (pbuh).

Day 59

Play a game

What to do

Play a game with your friend, father, brother or sister. Maybe you can play catch, Truth or Dare or Eye Spy.

Why?

Playing a game is the simplest joy in the day that will make you happy.

Allah...

Thank Allah for this happiness. '...*If you are grateful, I will certainly grant you more [favours]...*' - Quran 14:7.

Day 60
Focus on your blessings

What to do
Notice the good things in your life right now, even though some things might make you sad. You might have broken your favourite car, but you still have other cars. You might not have lots of friends but at least you have one.

Why?
When you focus on good things, your mind will forget the bad things, and you will feel happier.

Allah...
Allah says; *'certainly, with every hardship there is ease'* - Quran 94:5.

Day 61
Do your 5 prayers

What to do
Revolve your day around the worship of Allah by doing your 5 daily prayers. Maybe, wake up around Fajar time, lunch around Zohar, set playtime around Asar, homework around Magrib and sleep after Isha.

Why?
You were put on this Earth to worship, love and please Allah, so carrying out your purpose will give your heart peace and happiness.

Allah...
'I have not created jinn and mankind (for any purpose) except to worship Me' - Quran 51:56.

Day 62

Note a positive moment

What to do

Write down one positive thing that has happened to you in the last day. It might be that your father bought you a new pair of trainers? How do they look? How fast can you run? Read the note throughout the day.

Why?

When you write about good things, and keep reading them, your mind relives the good times and this will make you feel happy again.

Allah...

Thank Allah for this moment. He says *'...if you are grateful, I will certainly grant you more [favours]...'* - Quran 14:7.

Day 63
Be inspired by animals

What to do
Watch a nature programme. See how polar bears travel through Antarctica with their babies in search of food? Or how monkeys play with each other in the jungles?

Why?
Watching animal's lives will give you enjoyment and take your mind off worries.

Allah...
Subhan'Allah (glory be to Allah). *'And Allah has created every animal from water: of them there are some that crawl on their bellies; some that walk on two legs; and some that walk on four. Allah creates what He wills for verily Allah has power over all things'* - Quran 24:45.

Day 64
Meditate

What to do

Meditate for 10 minutes - switch off the lights, sit on the floor, with your hands on legs, close your eyes, breathe in for 2 seconds then release. With each breath say "Allah", reminding yourself that the reason your Lord keeps you alive and breathing is so you may worship Him.

Why?

This is a perfect way to step away from your busy life and bring peace to your mind.

Allah...

'Surely, in the remembrance of Allah do hearts find rest' - Quran 13:28.

Day 65
What do you like about yourself?

What to do

Think of one thing you like about yourself. Is it your humour, your sweet smile, your helpfulness, your intelligence? Remind yourself of this quality all day.

Why?

Thinking about your good qualities will make you feel good about yourself.

Allah...

Allah has given you lots of good qualities as gifts, *Alhamdulillah*. *'And if you were to count the blessings of Allah, never will you be able to count them'* - Quran 14:34.

Day 66
Life has happiness and sadness

What to do
Accept that life comes with both happiness and sadness for a reason. If it is dark, you will appreciate the light. If it is cold, you will be thankful when it is warm. When you are sad, you will be patient, trust Allah, and be grateful in happy times.

Why?
Being patient in sad times, and grateful in good times will make you a happier person.

Allah...
Allah will be pleased when you are patient and grateful. '...*If he (the believer) is granted ease of living, he is thankful; and this is best for him. And if he is afflicted with a hardship, he perseveres; and this is best for him*' - Prophet Muhammad (pbuh).

Day 67
Don't compare your life

What to do

Don't compare your life with anyone else's. Your friend might have a better bike than you, or your sister might have a better bedroom than you, that is Allah's choice. Focus on the good things you have.

Why?

Focussing on your blessings rather than looking at others, will give you peace and happiness.

Allah...

Allah says; 'do not strain your eyes in longing for the splendour that we have given to some groups to enjoy as a test for them. The provision of your Lord is better and more lasting' - Quran 20:131.

Day 68
Imagine the result

What to do
Are you working on something, like drawing a poster or learning to swim? Imagine how you would feel once it's done. Let the excitement keep you going.

Why?
The excitement of imagining you've completed your goal will make you happy.

Allah...
Also ask Allah for help with your goal, and He will. *'...indeed I am near. I answer the prayer of every caller (silent or audible) when he calls upon Me ...'* - Quran 2:186.

Day 69
You can choose happiness

What to do
Remember this; you can choose happiness by having a positive attitude. Say 'no' to negative thoughts like; if you're feeling tired or you don't want to do your homework. Think about the good things; your tasty chocolate bar or the cat you saw on the street.

Why?
If you think about good things only then you will feel happier.

Allah...
Allah is pleased when you are positive and don't complain; *'therefore remember Me. I will remember you. And be grateful to Me and do not be ungrateful'* - Quran 2:152.

Day 70
Look forward to Heaven

What to do

Do you know the best thing to look forward to is? Heaven. In Heaven you will; meet Allah, have lots of things and be happy. There will be no bad things. Think about it, ask Allah for it, and smile.

Why?

Looking forward to the great things in Heaven will make you excited and happy.

Allah...

'Say: "Shall I inform you of something better than that [worldly life]? For the righteous are Gardens by their Lord, beneath which rivers flow. There they shall live forever and [have] purified spouses and Allah's pleasure..."' - Quran 3:15.

Day 71
Draw things you enjoy

What to do
Draw the things that you enjoy doing and stick them to your wall. Do you like football, reading, going to the park, ice lollies?

Why?
When you see these pictures daily, it will remind you of happy moments and will make you feel happy.

Allah...
Thank Allah for your happy moments, which He will love. *'And if you were to count the blessings of Allah, never will you be able to count them'* - Quran 14:34.

Day 72
Your body is better than gold

What to do

Focus on your body. Think of how; your eyes allow you to see the beautiful world, your legs take you from the bed to the bathroom, your body stores food to give you the energy to learn and play. Where would you be without the parts on your body? Each one is worth more than a mountain of gold.

Why?

Thinking about your amazing body will make you feel so lucky and happy.

Allah...

Alhamdulillah for the great body Allah has given to you. *'Then which of your Lord's favours will you deny?'* - Quran 55:13.

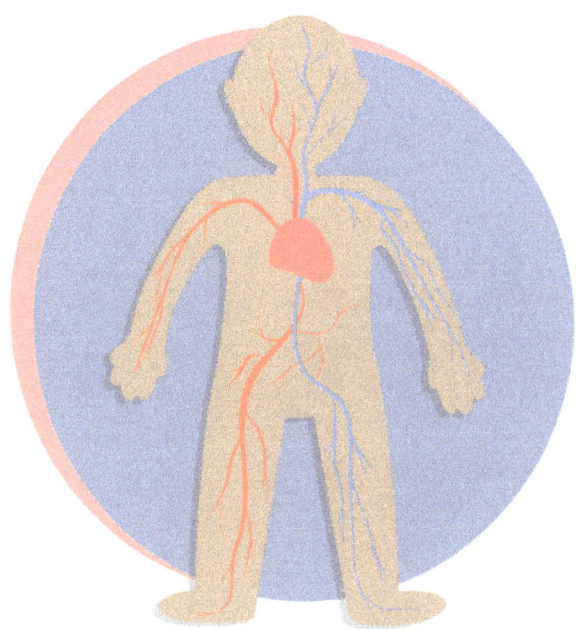

Day 73
Do things solely for Allah

What to do

Do good things for Allah. When sharing your play dough with your brother, do it because Allah will be pleased. When choosing not to cry for a toy, do it because you know Allah will be pleased with good behaviour.

Why?

When you are good, Allah will be pleased with you, other people will be pleased and you too will be pleased.

Allah...

'Allah will ask on the Day of Judgment: "Where are those who loved each other for the sake of My glory? Today – on a day when there is no shade but mine – I shall shade them with My shade"' - Prophet Muhammad (pbuh).

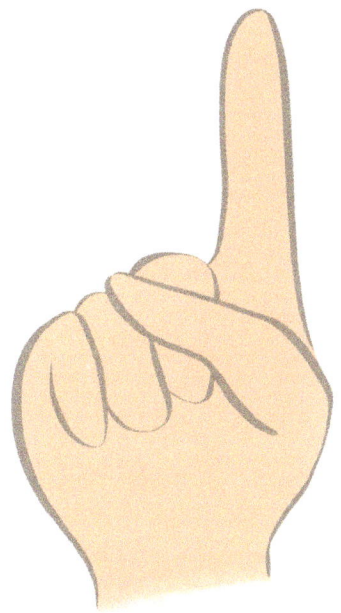

Day 74
Imagine you are not alive

What to do

Lie down for 10 minutes, with your eyes closed and imagine you are no longer alive. Imagine you've left behind your mother, your clothes, your bedroom.

Why?

It is a sad thought, but everyone will die one day. And remembering this will make you worry less, and you make you do your purpose of pleasing Allah by being good; which will lead to forever happiness in Heaven.

Allah...

Prophet Muhammad said. *'The one who remembers death most often and the one who is well-prepared to meet it; these are the wise; honorable in this life and dignified in the Hereafter.'*

Day 75
3 things you're grateful for

What to do
Write down 3 things you are grateful for. Maybe this is your lego set, your fun cousins or the fact that your mother reads to you every day?

Why?
When you are grateful you will be happier.

Allah...
Also, thank Allah for all these things He has given you – He will be pleased with you and give you even more. *'...If you are grateful, I will certainly grant you more [favours]...'* - Quran 14:7.

Day 76
Learn about human birth

What to do
Learn about how a baby is born. See how the baby grows and is born after exactly 9 months.

Why?
Learning something new and interesting will stop you from getting bored, amaze your mind and make you feel happy.

Allah....
Such learning will also show you how magnificent Allah is for creating this. *'Travel through the Earth and observe how Allah began creation. And then Allah will produce the final creation'* - Quran 29:20.

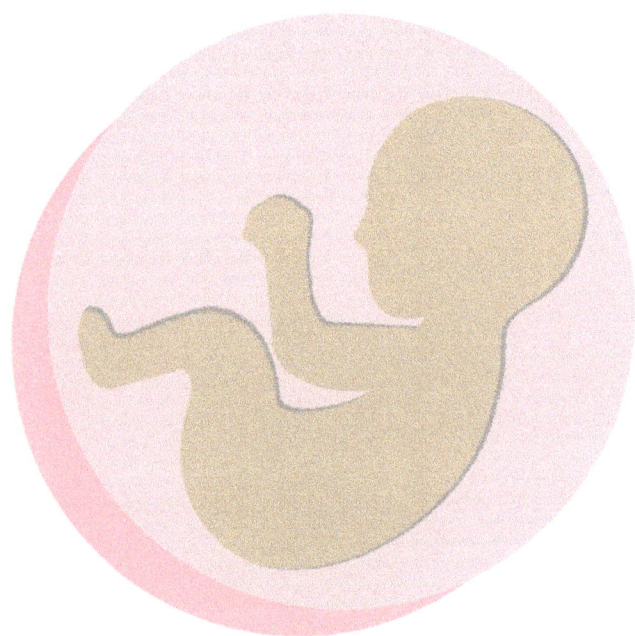

Day 77
Sleep the Islamic way

What to do

Sleep the Islamic way. Which is to sleep with ablution, lay on your right side. Recite *SubhanAllah* 33 times, *Alhamdulillah* 33 times, and *Allahu akbar* 34 times and blow over your body.

Why?

Prophet Muhammad (pbuh) said that will take away tiredness and energise you in the morning so much that it's better than having a servant.

Allah...

Allah will be pleased if you sleep remembering Him. *'And remember when He made slumber fall upon you as a means of serenity from Him'* - Quran 8:11.

Day 78
Write a thank you letter to Allah

What to do
Write a gratitude letter to Allah. Thank Allah for all He has given you. Explain how you love your tablet or how you have been given nice parents. There will be so many things to write about!

Why?
Writing this letter will show you how much you have to be happy about.

Allah...
Your thank you letter will please Allah and you'll be rewarded. *'And if you were to count the blessings of Allah, never will you be able to count them'* - Quran 14:34. *'...And Allah will soon reward the grateful ones'* - Quran 3: 144.

Day 79
Reject future worries

What to do
If you are worried about something - maybe going back to school, sitting your exam or not making friends at the mosque - then stop worrying. Do you know what will happen tomorrow? No. Will worrying help? No. Throw out all worried thoughts, and instead ask and trust Allah to do what is best for you.

Why?
Asking and trusting Allah will stop you worrying and feel happier.

Allah...
Prophe Muhammad said; *'what hit you, could not have missed you and what missed you could not have hit you'* and *'du'aa is the most potent weapon of a believer, it can change fate while no action of ours ever can'*.

Day 80
Chase Allah not the world

What to do

Stop chasing things, people, friends. These are temporary and will leave you or disappoint you one day. Chase Allah as He is the true source of wealth, respect and love. He is *al-Khaliq* (the Creator), *al-Wahhab* (the Giver of all), *al-Waddud* (the source of love). Run after Him, by praying, being kind, being thankful, and helping others.

Why?

Knowing that Allah will never leave and disappoint you will make you feel happy.

Allah...

Prophet Muhammad (pbuh) said *"Detach yourself from the world, and God will love you. Detach yourself from what is with the people, and the people will love you"*

Day 81
Talk to Allah

What to do

As you go through your day, talk to Allah. Allah is your Friend and you can chat to Him about anything. So as you enjoy your coco pops, say in your mind 'Allah, this is delicious thank you!' or if you are annoyed with your sister tell Allah why, and ask Him to help.

Why?

You will feel happier knowing that you have this Great, Helpful Friend with you all the time.

Allah...

Allah says; *'Call upon Me; I will respond to you'* - Quran 40:60

Day 82
Life is full of surprises

What to do

Look back at one thing that you would never have imagined would have happened – it might be your little brother being born, when only the day before he was not there? Or the surprise Eid present you got? Life is full of surprises.

Why?

It may be that a pleasant surprise will come your way again soon. Be hopeful.

Allah...

Anything is possible by the will of Allah; *'when He wills anything, His only command is to say "Be!" – and it is'*- Quran 36:82.

Day 83
Have a healthy meal

What to do

Ask an adult to help you with a healthy meal today. Maybe make a cucumber sandwich, or boiled veg with chicken? Avoid sugars, butter and fried food.

Why?

Eating healthy will make your body feel good, as well as your mind.

Allah...

Allah will be pleased when you look after your body; *'O mankind, Eat of what is lawful and wholesome on the Earth...'* - Quran 2:168.

Day 84
Be nice to 3 people

What to do

Do something nice for 3 people. Perhaps help your father in the kitchen? Tell your friend his shoes are nice? Share your candy with your grandmother? But don't expect things back. Do nice things because it pleases Allah and your purpose is to please Him.

Why?

Doing good things for nothing in return means you won't be disappointed by people and will be happy because Allah is happy.

Allah...

'We feed you for only Allah's pleasure. We desire no reward, nor thanks from you' - Quran 76:9.

Day 85
Plan a treat

What to do
Plan to treat yourself. Maybe you could have a cookie with your milk, or watch your favourite programme for half an hour after school.

Why?
Look forward to knowing a treat is coming, and really enjoy the pleasure it brings.

Allah...
Alhamdulillah for the simplest of blessings that Allah gives you every day; *'Then which of your Lord's favours will you deny?'* - Quran 55:13.

Day 86
Make decisions quickly

What to do
Make today's minor daily decisions quickly; like whether to have cereal or toast for breakfast, or whether to wear the red jumper or the blue one. Ask Allah to choose what's best for you, make a decision and don't look back.

Why?
Don't worry about small decisions, trust Allah and you will be happier.

Allah...
'Say: "Nothing shall ever happen to us except what Allah has ordained for us. He is our Mawla (protector)." And in Allah let the believers put their trust' - Quran 9:51.

Day 87

Plan a zoo trip

What to do

Plan a trip to the zoo. This is a great moment to reflect upon and marvel at the various animals that Allah has created; all in pairs – male and female.

Why?

Such amazement takes you away from the daily chores of life and brings happiness. Plan it and look forward to it.

Allah...

Did you know that every creature you see is busy in the worship of Allah? *'Do you not see that all within the Heavens and on Earth prostrate to Allah – the sun, the moon, the stars; the hills, the trees, the animals; and a great number of mankind?'* - Quran 22:18.

Day 88

Visit the cemetery

What to do

Visit the cemetery. Send blessings to the dead, they'll be grateful for it. Also, think about how one day you will go back to Allah.

Why?

Be happy knowing that all sadness in the world will end, and if you have been pleasing Allah in your life, then Allah and Heaven are waiting to welcome you.

Allah...

Prophet Muhammad (pbuh) told Muslims to visit cemetries as it will remind you of Allah, and that life is short, and Heaven is forever.

Day 89
Notice Allah's signs

What to do
Notice everything you see, feel, hear, touch and smell all day. These are signs of Allah – your dream at night, the sun in your eyes, the laughter of your friend.

Why?
Seeing Allah's signs will show you how kind, great and amazing He is. For this, you will love Him, worship Him and feel happy that He is everywhere around you.

Allah...
Allah says; *'Verily! In the creation of the Heavens and the Earth, and in the alternation of night and day, there are indeed signs for those who have intelligence'* - Quran 3:190.

Day 90
Pause, scan and thank Allah

What to do

As often as you can today, pause, scan your surroundings and think of your blessings at that moment. Your smart leather jacket, your tasty lunch, your loving family, the sun shining through your windows? With each thought, thank Allah by saying *alhamdulillah*.

Why?

When you are grateful, your heart will feel happiness.

Allah...

Allah will love you for being grateful and will give you more; *'... If you are grateful, I will certainly grant you more [favours]...'* - Quran 14:7.

Day 91
Money doesn't make you happier

What to do

It is a fact that having lots of money doesn't make you happier. Having enough money for decent food, shelter and clothing is important but once you have that, having a shiny bike rather than a rusty one doesn't make you that much happier. Your positive mind is what makes a difference.

Why?

Knowing this will stop you wanting more and give your heart peace.

Allah...

'True enrichment does not come through possessing a lot of wealth, but true enrichment is the enrichment of the soul' - Prophet Muhammad (pbuh).

Day 92
Think of 5 people less fortunate

What to do
Think about 5 people that are less fortunate than you in some ways. Maybe someone who does not have a sister, or someone who broke their knee recently?

Why?
Thinking about this will make you feel grateful and happier about yourself.

Allah...
'Look at those below you (less fortunate than you), and do not look at those above you, for this is better' - Prophet Muhammad (pbuh).

Day 93
Recite Surah Yaseen

What to do
Recite *surah Yaseen* (Quran, chapter 36) this morning.

Why?
By reciting this special chapter of the Quran in the morning, it will bring peace and blessings into your whole day, *insha'Allah*.

Allah...
'Everything has a heart and the heart of the Quran is surah Yaseen, whoever reads surah Yaseen, Allah will write the reward of reading the Quran ten times from him'; 'it takes away from its reader all afflictions and fulfils his needs for the day' - Prophet Mohammed (pbuh).

Day 94
Fulfil your purpose today

What to do

Carry out your life's purpose today; which is worshipping Allah. So do things that please Him; make your prayers, be grateful for good, trust Him in bad times, be kind, share, don't argue or do bad, and look forward to Heaven.

Why?

Doing your life's purpose is what will give your heart peace and happiness.

Allah...

Allah says; *'I have not created jinn and mankind (for any purpose) except to worship Me'* - Quran 51:56

Day 95
Have a clear out

What to do

Get rid of clutter; things you haven't used in a year, or don't need. Books, toys, crafts. Give them away to charity or throw them away. Don't feel that you might need it one day, live for today and trust in Allah for tomorrow.

Why?

Having too many things will give you stress. Living simply and also giving to the poor, will make you feel happy.

Allah...

Prophet Muhammad (pbuh) said: *'the son of Adam will not pass away from Allah until he is asked about five things...'*, the fourth being; *'how did he spend his wealth...'*

Day 96
Know your final destination

What to do

As you walk along any path, there is always a destination; school, home, the shop. Life's final destination is the Hereafter. As you walk today, happily or sadly, to wherever, know that this walk is eventually leading to the Hereafter and to Allah.

Why?

Remembering this will make you look forward to the day you are walking through Heaven and meeting Allah, *insha'Allah*.

Allah...

'*Surely, to Allah we belong, and to Him we shall return*' - Quran 2:156.

Day 97
Have some alone time

What to do
Have an hour to do whatever you want today – read, watch TV, pamper yourself, pray, play. Be yourself for this hour.

Why?
Alone time is important for emotional, spiritual and social health – which will make you happier.

Allah...
Alhamdulillah for the simple alone time Allah has gifted you; 'Then which of your Lord's favours will you deny?' - Quran 55:13.

Day 98
Gaze at the stars

What to do
Tonight, step outside and look up. Gaze at the stars for at least 15 minutes. Forget about everything else but the wonders of these twinkling beads. Make a wish to Allah. Believe that the wish will come true.

Why?
Believing that there is something greater than anything on Earth will make you feel happier.

Allah...
'And it is He who ordained the stars for you that you may be guided thereby in the darkness of the land and the sea' - Quran 6:97.

Day 99

Note a positive moment

What to do

Write down one positive thing that has happened to you in the last day. It might be that you passed an exam; how hard did you work? Did you laugh when you passed? Did you tell your friends? Read the note throughout the day.

Why?

When you write about good things, and keep reading them, your mind relives the good times and this will make you feel happy again.

Allah...

Thank Allah for this moment. He says '...*if you are grateful, I will certainly grant you more [favours]...*' - Quran 14:7.

> **Positive Moment of the Last Day:**
>
> I had a great time bike riding with Rahma yesterday. We went really fast down the hills in the park and it was amazing!

Day 100
Write 'B' for Bismillah

What to do

Write a 'B' on the back of your hand. 'B' for *bismillah* (in the name of Allah). Every time you see the B, say *bismillah* before every activity you begin; putting your clothes on, getting into the car, eating dinner.

Why?

Saying *bismillah* will bring Allah's blessing into your tasks and remind you of your purpose. Your heart will feel peace.

Allah...

Allah will be pleased that everything you are doing is in His name; *'I have not created jinn and mankind (for any purpose) except to worship Me'* - Quran 51:56.

Day 101
Hardships are good for you

What to do

When something bad happens, realise that it may be for the best. Perhaps you got late for school, because Allah wanted to save you from an accident. Maybe you fell ill because Allah wanted to teach you to be patient with Him and to be grateful when you feel better.

Why?

Always thinking that if anything bad happens, it could be for the best, will make you feel better.

Allah...

'...And it may be that you dislike a thing which is good for you and that you like a thing which is bad for you. Allah knows but you do not know' - Quran 2:216.

Day 102
Enjoy the world's beauty

What to do
Search for some photos online of beautiful natural places in this world. The Maldives, Amazon rainforest, Northern Lights? Enjoy them, but know that Heaven promises much more.

Why?
Smile and be excited to see the amazing beauties in Heaven one day, *insha'Allah*.

Allah...
Ask Allah to show you Heaven. '... *In Heaven, there will be whatever the heart desires, whatever pleases the eye ...*' - Quran 43:71.

Day 103
3 things you're grateful for

What to do
Write down 3 things you are grateful for. Maybe it's the bike ride you went on earlier, or the strawberry milkshake you made, or the bird that flew into your garden?

Why?
When you are grateful you will be happier.

Allah...
Also, thank Allah for all these things He has given you – He will be pleased with you and give you even more. '...*If you are grateful, I will certainly grant you more [favours]...*' - Quran 14:7.

1. My Mummy

2. Cheerios

3. My colourful socks

Day 104
Be a slave to only Allah

What to do

Be a slave to Allah, and not a slave to people or things. Don't let money, friends, popularity control your thoughts and actions. Make Allah your purpose by doing things that please Him; be kind, share, don't argue, don't complain, pray, be patient, be grateful.

Why?

When you stop feeling like a slave to everything other than Allah, you will feel free and happy, as your eternal happiness is with Allah.

Allah...

'Say, "Indeed, my prayer, my acts of worship, my life and my death are for Allah, Lord of the worlds"' - Quran 6:162.

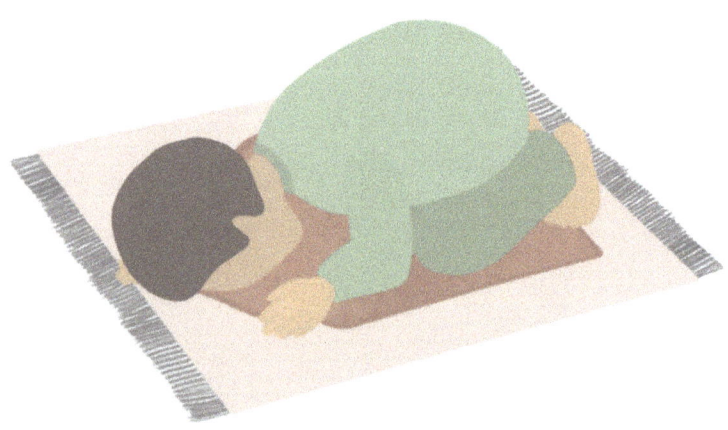

Day 105
Sleep enough

What to do
Have 8 hours sleep tonight. Turn off your gadgets, put your toys away, hug your pillow, and close your eyes.

Why?
Sleep is very important for your mind and body to feel happy and energised the next day. And it is worth more than $60,000 a year!

Allah...
Alhamdulillah for the gift of sleep. *'And remember when He made slumber fall upon you as a means of serenity from Him'* - Quran 8:11.

Day 106
Accept Allah's decisions

What to do
Accept all that Allah has decided for you. The size of your room, number of your friends, colour of your skin. Allah is the most-wise, makes the best decisions and He knows what is good for you. So be grateful, be patient and trust Allah to be doing what is best for you.

Why?
Accepting Allah's decisions about your life will make you feel at peace.

Allah...
This will also please Allah. *'Say: "Nothing shall ever happen to us except what Allah has ordained for us. He is our Mawla (protector)" And in Allah let the believers put their trust'* - Quran 9:51.

Day 107
Have a relaxing bath

What to do
Have a nice warm bath today. Relax, put some bubbles in and play with the water.

Why?
Baths are a relaxing treat that will bring you happiness.

Allah...
Alhamdulillah for this wonderful gift Allah has given you; *'Then which of your Lord's favours will you deny?'* - Quran 55:13.

Day 108

Be amazed by life under water

What to do

Watch a nature programme on creatures that live in the sea. Be amazed by dolphins, sharks, fish or crabs.

Why?

Watching other creatures lives will give you enjoyment and take your mind off worries.

Allah...

Subhan'Allah (glory be to Allah). 'And Allah has created every animal from water: of them there are some that crawl on their bellies; some that walk on two legs; and some that walk on four. Allah creates what He wills for verily Allah has power over all things' - Quran 24:45.

Day 109
Give dinner to neighbours

What to do
Share some of your dinner with your neighbour. Invite them round or give them a plateful.

Why?
This good deed will make you and your neighbour feel happy.

Allah...
Allah will also be pleased with you; *'Whenever you prepare a broth, put plenty of water in it, and give some to your neighbours and then give them out of this with courtesy'*, said Prophet Muhammad (pbuh).

Day 110

Are you positive or negative?

What to do

Are you a positive or negative person? When you look at the sky, do you see the clouds or the sun behind them? Do you see a glass half full or half empty? If you are negative, then become positive.

Why?

By looking at the positive side of all things, you will be happier.

Allah...

Being positive will also please Allah; '...*if you are grateful, I will certainly grant you more [favours]...*' - Quran 14:7.

Day 111
Do some exercise

What to do

Do some exercise today. Brisk march up and down your street, run around your house, skate in your garden.

Why?

Scientists say that exercise is very important for happiness, as when you exercise, chemicals are sent to your brain that make you feel happy. Exercise also makes you healthier, look trimmer, think better and sleep well.

Allah...

Thank Allah for gifting you a healthy body to exercise; *'Then which of your Lord's favours will you deny?'* - Quran 55:13.

Day 112
Treat all like it's their last day

What to do
Treat everyone you meet as if they will no longer be here tomorrow, because they might not be. Be extremely kind and caring to your family, friends, teacher, the shopkeeper. Smile, listen, be nice. Don't expect anything back.

Why?
They will be happy and you will feel happy.

Allah...
Most of all, Allah will be pleased; '*...and do good (to others); surely Allah loves the doers of good*' - Quran 2:195.

Day 113
Think about achievements

What to do
Think about one of your achievements from the past year. Have you learnt to; bake, ride a bike, swim? Think about how this may help your future.

Why?
You are accomplished and have done well. Feel happy.

Allah...
Alhamdulillah for your achievements; *'And if you were to count the blessings of Allah, never will you be able to count them'* - Quran 14:34.

Day 114
Have a meaningful chat

What to do

Have a deep conversation with someone. Discuss the purpose of life? The beliefs of various religions? World poverty? The meaning of happiness?

Why?

Having meaningful conversations will improve your happiness.

Allah...

Such conversations may also remind you of Allah. *'Verily! In the creation of the Heavens and the Earth, and in the alternation of night and day, there are indeed signs for those who have intelligence'* - Quran 3:190.

Day 115
Smile and say salaams

What to do
Give a friend, family member, class mate and stranger one of your smiles and say; *assalamu'alaikum* (may peace be upon you). They might be in need of this smile and prayer.

Why?
A smile is contagious, so your smile might make them smile, and will certainly make your heart smile.

Allah...
Allah will be pleased with your kindness; *'to smile in the face of your brother is charity given on your behalf'* - Prophet Muhammad.

Day 116
Forgive others

What to do
Are you feeling angry with anyone? Maybe with your brother for using up your paints, or with your friend for tripping you up at school. If you are, then forgive them.

Why?
Being angry is a wasteful feeling and will make your heart heavy. Forgiveness cleans your soul and mind; and you'll feel much happier for it.

Allah...
Allah will also be pleased: *'whoever will not show mercy, will not be shown mercy by Allah'* - Prophet Muhammad.

Day 117
Escape the world with prayer

What to do
When you step onto your prayer mat, mentally step away from the world, and devote this moment of love to your Creator. Forget about what else is going on and remind yourself of your purpose in life; which is to please Allah.

Why?
This is a great moment of peace. A meeting between you and Allah. And it is your soul's truest joy.

Allah...
'Surely, in the remembrance of Allah do hearts find rest' - Quran 13:28.

Day 118
Contact a good friend

What to do
Meet or call a good friend. A good friend is a good person, who is positive, doesn't complain and argue, and shows happiness.

Why?
Friendship with good people is one of life's greatest joy, as their good vibes will spread to you.

Allah...
Prophet Muhammad's (pbuh) advice is to keep good friends *'whose appearance reminds you of God, and whose speech increases you in knowledge, and whose actions remind you of the Hereafter'*.

Day 119
3 things you love about you

What to do

Write down 3 things that you love about yourself. Your smile? Your accent? Your humour? Your eyes? Your fitness? Your ambition? Your kindness? Remind yourself of these 3 traits throughout the day.

Why?

Loving yourself and being thankful for you, will make you happier.

Allah...

Alhamdulillah for how Allah has made you; *'And if you were to count the blessings of Allah, never will you be able to count them'* - Quran 14:34.

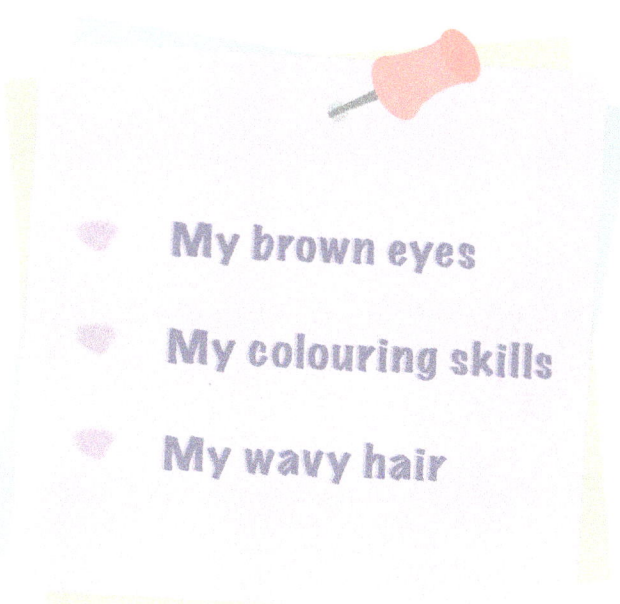

Day 120
You are one of the luckiest

What to do

You are very lucky. You have what 80% of the world does not have if you have; a roof over your head, a warm bed to sleep in, food and drink whenever you want, nice clothes and an education in English. Think about the things you have that most children in the world do not have.

Why?

When you are grateful, you are happier.

Allah...

Alahmdulillah for being one of the luckiest; *'And if you were to count the blessings of Allah, never will you be able to count them'* - Quran 14:34.

Day 121
Get a plant

What to do

Get a plant to put in your room. Watch this beautiful life grow. Just like people and animals, plants live and die, fight amongst each other, compete for mates, reproduce and travel, but the drama is a lot slower.

Why?

A plant in your room will amaze you daily, reduce stress and give you enjoyment.

Allah...

Did you know that even plants are in constant worship of Allah? *'...Behold, verily in these things there are signs for those who understand!'* - Quran 13:4.

Day 122
Face smile and heart smile

What to do
Put a smile on your face often today, but also put a smile on your heart by doing something good. Perhaps take some bread to the nearest pond and feed the ducks or say hello to your lonely neighbour.

Why?
A smile on your face and a good deed will make your heart smile.

Allah...
Allah will be pleased with your good act '*...And do good (to others); surely Allah loves the doers of good*' - Quran 2:195.

Day 123
Note a positive moment

What to do

Write down one positive thing that has happened to you in the last day. It might be your first swimming lesson; was it fun? What did you do? Who did you splash? Read the note throughout the day.

Why?

When you write about good things, and keep reading them, your mind relives the good times and this will make you feel happy again.

Allah...

Thank Allah for this moment. He says '...*if you are grateful, I will certainly grant you more [favours]...*' - Quran 14:7.

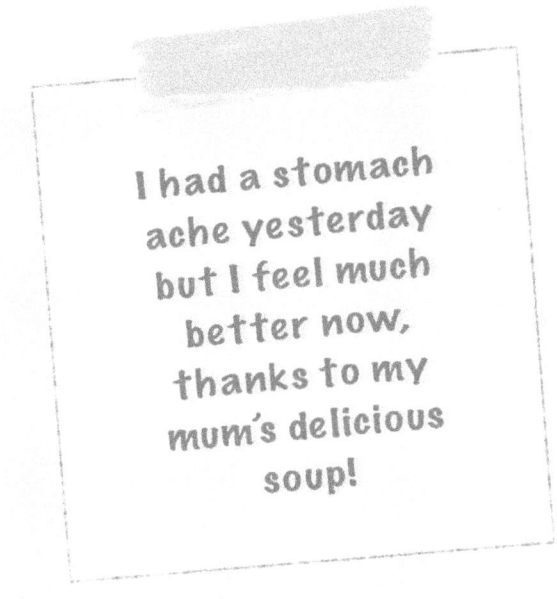

Day 124
Ask Allah for your hopes

What to do
Ask Allah for whatever you hope for. Do you want to be clever? Enjoy dinner? Allah is the Giver and Taker of everything. Ask Him for something, and He will give it to you in some way or another. Du'aa (asking Allah) is your strongest power in the world.

Why?
Be happy knowing you have this special power called 'du'aa'.

Allah…
'Du'aa is the most potent weapon of a believer, it can change fate while no action of ours ever can' - Prophet Muhammad (pbuh).

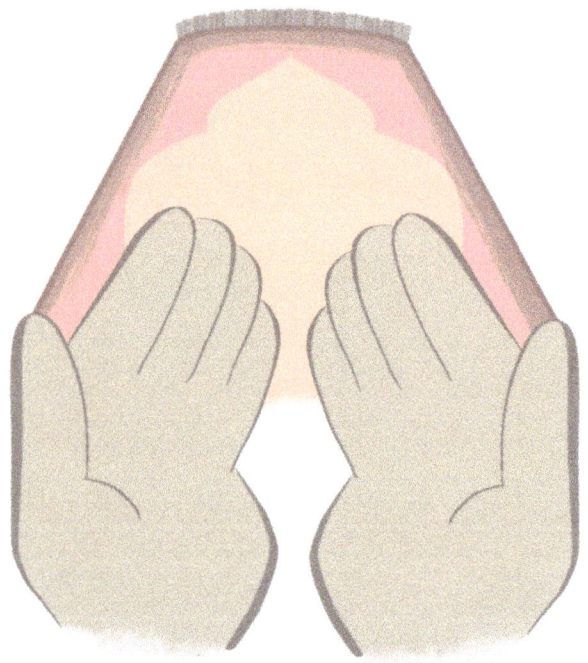

Day 125
Plant 100 trees in Heaven

What to do
Say; *'subhanAllah il azeem wa bi hamdihi'* (glory and praise be to Allah, the Almighty) 100 times. Each time you say it Allah plants a huge palm tree for you in Heaven. A tree so big that it would take a horse 40 years to ride around its shade. Make yourself a magnificent forest!

Why?
Look forward to one day visiting your new trees in Heaven, *insha'Allah*.

Allah...
'When He wills anything, His only command is to say "Be!" – and it is'- Quran 36:82.

Day 126
5 things you want in Heaven

What to do

Write down 5 things that you dream to have. Do you want; a house made of diamonds? Servants serving you all day? A giant trampoline? Ask Allah for it and truly believe you will have them in Heaven.

Why?

Heaven is real, and one day you will have all these things plus more! Smile and look forward to it.

Allah...

Allah says '... *In Heaven, there will be whatever the heart desires, whatever pleases the eye ....*' - Quran 43:71.

Day 127
Start chasing a dream

What to do
Think of something you've always wanted to do. Like learn to skate, learn Spanish, write a book, build a robot? Start doing it or planning it now.

Why?
Having dreams and ambitions will give you new excitement and enjoyment in life.

Allah...
Before you begin, say *bismillah* (in the name of Allah) and ask Allah to help; *'You alone do we worship and You alone do we seek for help'* - Quran 1:5.

Day 128
Don't take bad things personally

What to do
Don't take the bad things that other people do or say to you personally. When people are mean, it is more about them than you. Maybe they've had a bad day or a hard upbringing.

Why?
Some people will be kind to you, some will not - forgive the mean ones and you'll be happier.

Allah...
'Allah will ask on the Day of Judgment: "Where are those who loved each other for the sake of My glory? Today – on a day when there is no shade but mine – I shall shade them with My shade"' - Prophet Muhammad (pbuh).

Day 129
Understand the Quran

What to do
Read the translation of a sentence in the Quran.

Why?
These are the direct words of Allah and you will feel closer to Him when you understand His book. And when you feel close to Allah, your heart is happier.

Allah...
'Surely, in the remembrance of Allah do hearts find rest' - Quran 13:28.

Day 130
Inspire others with positivity

What to do
Make others feel good by being positive, upbeat and saying only nice things.

Why?
People will love you for your positivity and want to be around you. And whilst spreading happy vibes to others, you are spreading them to yourself too.

Allah...
Allah will be pleased with your positivity; *'Blessed is the person who speaks good...'* - Prophet Muhammad (pbuh).

Day 131
Plan a fun day

What to do
Plan a fun day and put a date in; maybe a garden party with your friends, or a trip to the park with your cousins?

Why?
Now you have something to look forward to and that will make you feel happy.

Allah...
Alhamdulillah for fun days; *'Then which of your Lord's favours will you deny?'* - Quran 55:13.

Day 132
Remember Allah

What to do

Remember Allah and He will remember you. Say 'Allah' when you wake up, say 'subhan'Allah' when you see a pretty bird, say 'sorry Allah' when you do something wrong, say 'bismillah' when you start something, say 'Alhamdulillah' at the end of the day.

Why?

The most important thing you need in life to give you peace and happiness, is Allah – your Creator, Sustainer and Destroyer. Love Him and He will love you. Please Him and He will please you.

Allah...

'...Remember Me. I will remember you...' - Quran 2:152.

Day 133
Do acts of charity

What to do
Be charitable all day today. Charity does not mean just giving money, it could mean being nice, helpful, positive.

Why?
Allah will be pleased, people will be pleased and you will be pleased.

Allah...
Prophet Muhammad (pbuh) said; *'to smile in the company of your brother is charity. To command to do good deeds and to prevent others from doing evil is charity. To guide a person in a place where he cannot get astray is charity. To remove troublesome things like thorns and bones from the road is charity. To pour water from your jug into the jug of your brother is charity. To guide a person with defective vision is charity for you'.*

Day 134
Be patient in your day

What to do

Throughout the day write 10 things that aren't how you want them to be. Your loneliness? Your cold room? Your burnt toast? Each time you write something, smile bravely, think how it could be worse, be patient, trust Allah and say *alhamdulillah*.

Why?

Half of happiness is to be patient in hard times, by accepting and trusting Allah's decisions.

Allah…

Allah will be pleased with your patience and reward you; *'I have rewarded them this day for their patience and faithfulness: they are indeed the ones that have achieved bliss…'* - Quran 23:111.

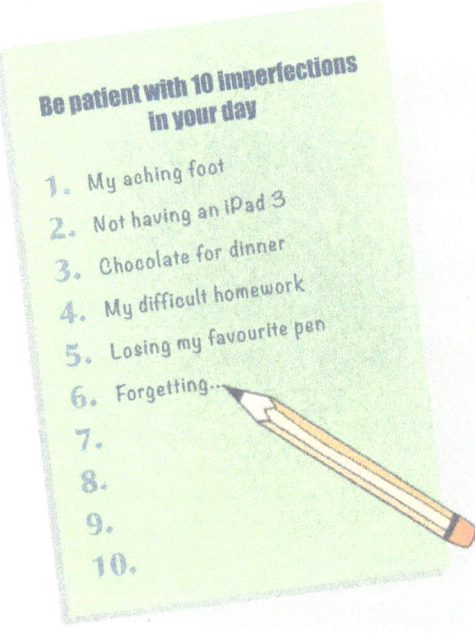

Day 135
3 things you're grateful for

What to do

Write down 3 things you are grateful for. Maybe it's the ladybird you got to play with in the garden, the cool ice lolly you ate, the funky socks you're wearing?

Why?

When you are grateful for what you have, you will be happier.

Allah...

Also, thank Allah for all these things He has given you – He will be pleased with you and give you even more. '...*If you are grateful, I will certainly grant you more [favours]...*' - Quran 14:7.

Day 136

Go out into nature

What to do

Go out somewhere nice, like the park, beach or riverside. Run, walk, skip. Breathe in the fresh air, feel the wind on your face, and hear the birds.

Why?

Fresh air and daylight will refresh your mind and body, and make you feel happier.

Allah...

Notice the amazing world Allah has created *'...And they think deeply about the creation of the Heavens and the Earth, [saying] "Our Lord! You did not create (all) of this without a purpose, glory be to You"...'* - Quran 3:191.

Day 137
Accept Allah's decisions

What to do
Accept all that Allah has decided. Your height, your parents, your simple clothes. Allah is the most-wise, makes the best decisions and He knows what is good for you. So be grateful, be patient and trust Allah to be doing what is best for you.

Why?
Accepting Allah's decisions about your life will make you feel at peace.

Allah...
This will also please Allah. *'...And it may be that you dislike a thing which is good for you and that you like a thing which is bad for you. Allah knows but you do not know'* - Quran 2:216.

Day 138
Organise your room

What to do
Organise and tidy your bedroom. Minimise clutter, put bits and bats away, file papers, hang clothes up, hoover up, wipe surfaces clean, throw out unused items.

Why?
It is important to keep your surroundings clutter free, orderly and clean so that your mind feels calm and at peace.

Allah...
'And Allah has made for you from your homes a place of rest' - Quran 16:80.

Day 139
Slowdown in your prayers

What to do

Slowdown in your prayers and concentrate. Allah is your Master, your Creator and Destroyer. There is nothing in your life right now that is more important than Him. So take your time in your worship of Him, focus on the words you are reciting and the reasons behind your bows, and feel your love for Allah.

Why?

For your soul, you connecting and pleasing Allah is the truest joy.

Allah...

'Do not rush your salah for anything, as you're standing infront of the One who is in control of whatever you are rushing for' - Unknown.

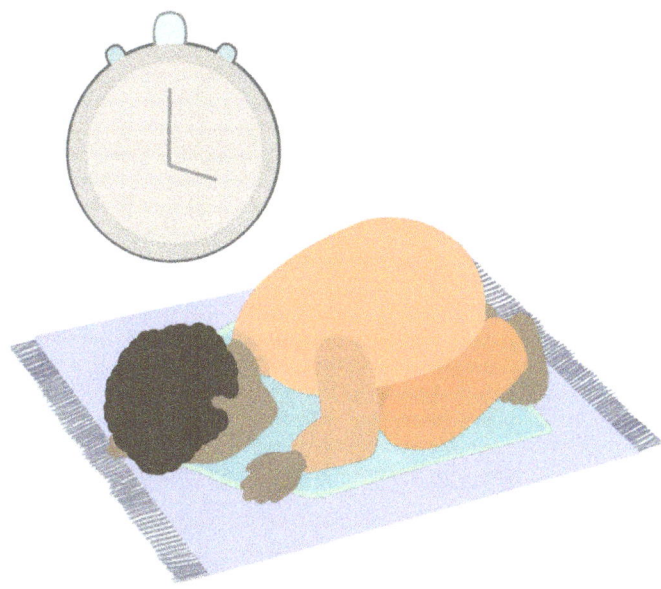

Day 140
Write a secret note

What to do
Write a secret note to a loved one; you mother, aunty, friend? Write about how lovely you think they are and then hide the note in their pocket for them to see later.

Why?
You will make someone smile today, as well as yourself.

Allah...
Allah will be pleased with your sweet act. *'Blessed is the person who speaks good...'* - Prophet Muhammad (pbuh).

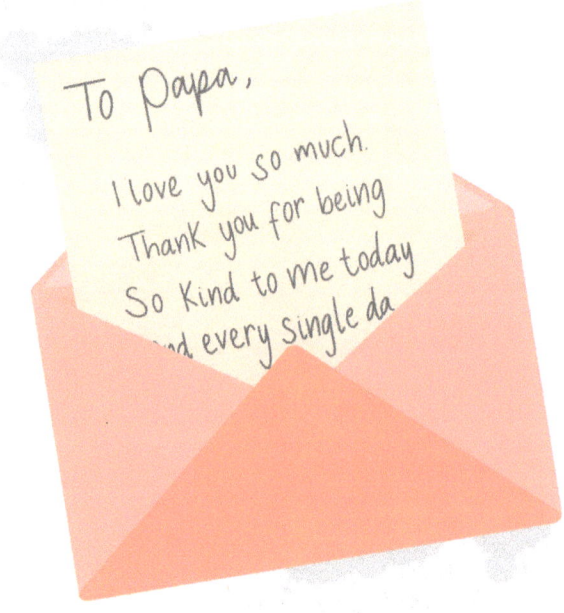

Day 141
Imagine being a poor orphan

What to do

Every time you eat today, imagine you are a poor orphan who cannot afford the food you are about to eat – an apple pie, chocolate bar, beef steak, chips, chicken curry, fresh orange juice. Picture the food you would be eating instead – bread, water, scraps. Imagine the hunger you would feel.

Why?

Appreciate what Allah has given you. You have too much to be happy about.

Allah...

Alhamdulillah; '*So take what I have given you and be of the grateful ones*' - Quran 7:144.

Day 142
Give good advice

What to do
Give some good advice to others today. You could flick through this book, pick out a tip that you have found useful, and share it with your friends and family.

Why?
By helping someone, you will naturally feel good.

Allah...
Allah will be pleased with you; 'Allah and His angels, and the inhabitants of the Heavens and the Earth, even the ant in its hole, and even the fish, send blessings upon the one who teaches people good things' - Prophet Muhammad (pbuh).

> Did you know, you are luckier than millions of other children in the world?

Day 143
Feed an animal

What to do
Give food to an animal today. Birds, ducks, pigeons, fish, cats, bees, or even ants. Give some bread, sugar or milk.

Why?
This nice act will give happiness to the animal and will make you feel good.

Allah...
Allah will be pleased with you too; *'You shall be rewarded for kindness to every living thing'* - Prophet Muhammad (pbuh).

Day 144
Zoom in on good things

What to do
Zoom in on the good things in your life right now; your caring mother, your cosy sofa, your healthy eyes. And zoom out of the bad things - don't think about them.

Why?
When you focus on good things, your mind will forget the bad things, and you will feel happier.

Allah...
Allah says; *'certainly, with every hardship there is ease'* - Quran 94:5, *'and if you were to count the blessings of Allah, never will you be able to count them'* - Quran 14:34.

Day 145
Remember your purpose in life

What to do
Whenever you feel sad, pause for a minute, close your eyes and remind yourself of your purpose; "I am here to please Allah". So act on it; be nice to others, pray, be thankful, don't complain, remember Allah.

Why?
Don't worry about anything that is not relevant to your purpose and your day will be much happier.

Allah...
Allah will be pleased; *'I have not created jinn and mankind (for any purpose) except to worship Me'* - Quran 51:56.

Day 146
Avoid eating too much

What to do

Don't eat too much. Follow Prophet Muhammad's (pbuh) advice. Let a third of your stomach be filled with food, a third with water, and a third with air.

Why?

Eating too much can make you feel sick, sleepy, lazy, put on weight and is also, not Islamic.

Allah...

'And eat and drink, but waste not in extravagance, certainly He (Allah) does not like those who waste' - Quran 7:31.

Day 147

Note a positive moment

What to do

Write down one positive thing that has happened to you in the last day. It might be that you managed to do a handstand- how long did you do it for? Who was there to watch? Did you feel great? Read the note throughout the day.

Why?

When you write about good things, and keep reading them, your mind relives the good times and this will make you feel happy again.

Allah...

Thank Allah for this moment. He says '...*if you are grateful, I will certainly grant you more [favours]...*' - Quran 14:7.

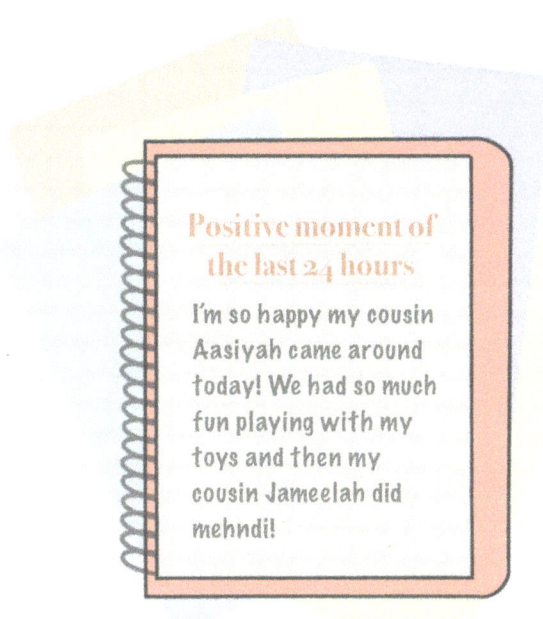

Day 148
Trust Allah like the bird does

What to do

Look up at the sky and watch the birds looking for food. They trust Allah to take care of them. Be like that bird. Say 'I trust you Allah' and believe He will look after you too.

Why?

By trusting Allah to take care of you, you will feel happy.

Allah...

Prophet Muhammed (pbuh) said; *'If you were to rely upon Allah with the reliance He is due, you would be given provision like the birds: They go out hungry in the morning and come back with full bellies in the evening'*.

Day 149
Life on Earth is a short stop

What to do

Remember, life is a temporary pit stop. Life is a journey from Allah to Allah. You came from Allah, are spending some time on Earth, then will go back to Allah - to your forever home.

Why?

Remembering this will help you not worry too much about life and problems in the day. You will feel much happier.

Allah...

'Surely, to Allah we belong, and to Him we shall return' - Quran 2:156. *'Be in this world as though you are a traveller'* - Prophet Muhammad (pbuh).

Day 150
Feed a homeless person

What to do
Make a sandwich and give it to a local homeless person today. Imagine what it would be like to be homeless.

Why?
You will feel happy knowing you've made someone else happy, and also, that you have a home.

Allah...
Allah will be pleased at your kindness and thankfulness; *'And if you were to count the blessings of Allah, never will you be able to count them'* - Quran 14:34.

Day 151
Do some exercise

What to do

Do 30 minutes of exercise today. You could follow an online workout video. By the end of it, you should be mentally and physically energised.

Why?

Scientists say that exercise is very important for happiness as when you exercise, chemicals are sent to your brain that make you feel happy. Exercise also makes you healthier, look trimmer, think better and sleep well.

Allah...

Allah will be pleased if you look after the body He has gifted you with; *'Then which of your Lord's favours will you deny?'* - Quran 55:13.

Day 152
Do something you used to do

What to do

Do something you used to do when you were very young. Zoom around your living room with toy cars, have a tea party with your imaginary friend?

Why?

You will feel the fun and happiness of your childhood again.

Allah...

Also, you may not have said thank you to Allah when you were little so you can now, *alhamdulillah*. *'And if you were to count the blessings of Allah, never will you be able to count them'* - Quran 14:34.

Day 153
Allah will test you

What to do

Know that your life will always have sadness sometimes. Allah will test you (and everyone else) all your life, to see if you will be patient with Allah, trust Him, and still love Him. Prophet Muhammad was tested lots!

Why?

Be accepting of sad times. And be happy knowing that if you stay patient, trust Allah and still please Him, Heaven will be your reward.

Allah...

'Most definitely We will test you with some fear and hunger, some loss in goods, lives and the fruits (of your toil)...' - Quran 2:155.

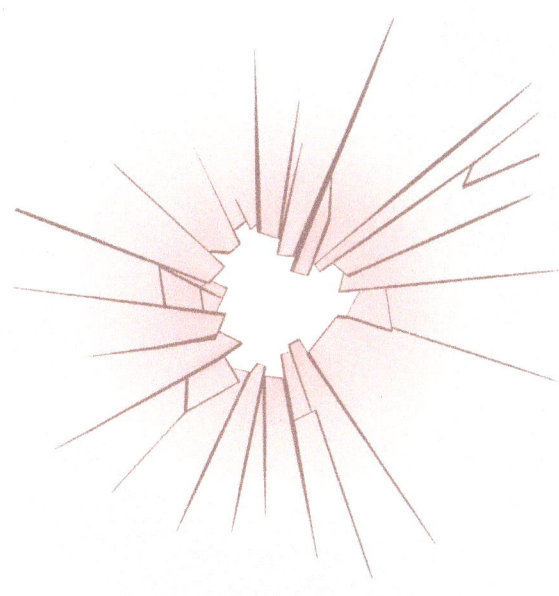

Day 154
Eat fruit and veg

What to do
Eat 5 portions of fruit or vegetables. Make a juice, smoothie or a salad lunch.

Why?
Eating healthy will make your body feel good, as well as your mind.

Allah...
Allah will be pleased when you look after your body; *'O mankind, Eat of what is lawful and wholesome on the Earth...'* - Quran 2:168.

Day 155
Meditate

What to do

Meditate for 10 minutes - switch off the lights, sit on the floor, with your hands on your legs, close your eyes, breathe in for 2 seconds then release. With each breath say 'Allah', reminding yourself that the reason your Lord keeps you alive and breathing is so you may worship Him.

Why?

This is a perfect way to step away from your busy life and bring peace to your mind.

Allah...

'Surely, in the remembrance of Allah do hearts find rest' - Quran 13:28.

Day 156
Do something nice

What to do

Do something nice for someone today. Say a kind word to a stranger. Share your lunch with your friend. Greet the neighbour with the Islamic prayer, *assalamu'alaikum warahmatullahi wabarakatuh* (may the peace, mercy, and blessings of Allah be with you).

Why?

When you do nice things for people, they will feel happy and you will feel happy.

Allah...

Also, Allah will be happy with you; *'Whoever does good equal to the weight of an atom (or a small ant), shall see it'* - Quran 99:7.

Day 157
Heaven has forever happiness

What to do
Don't expect too much from the world, as it was never meant to be perfect. Your soul came from Allah, and it is only when it returns to Allah in perfect Heaven will it find true happiness.

Why?
So put your heart at ease when things go wrong in life, and be happy that one day you will have forever happiness.

Allah...
Allah says; *'Oh mankind, indeed you are ever toiling towards your Lord, painfully toiling... But you shall meet Him'* - Quran 84:6.

Day 158
Write a gratitude list

What to do

Write down all the things you are grateful for. This could be; the soft bed that you wake up in, the nice words your aunty says to you, your red bicycle, the delicious chicken nuggets you have for dinner.

Why?

When you are grateful you will be happier.

Allah...

Also, thank Allah for all these things He has given you – He will be pleased with you and give you even more. '...*If you are grateful, I will certainly grant you more [favours]...*' - Quran 14:7.

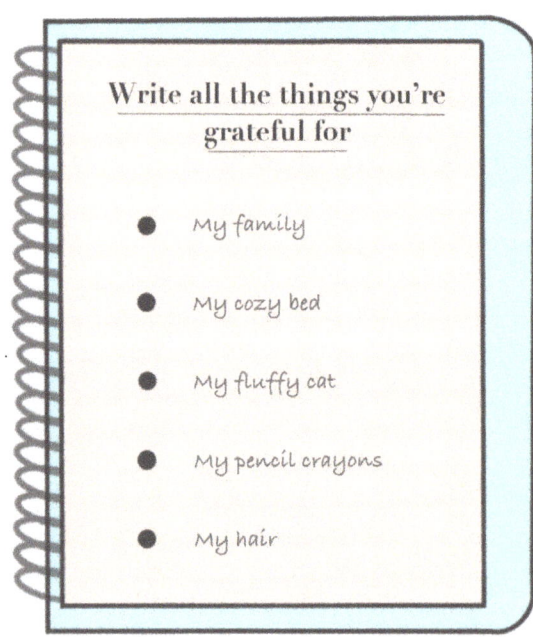

Day 159
Allah is worthy of your life

What to do
Have full belief in the testimony of Islam, the Shahada; *'Laa illaha illallahu muhammadur rasoolullah'* (There is no diety worthy of worship except Allah, and Muhammad (pbuh) is His messenger). Nothing is worth your hope, fear, love, tears except Allah.

Why?
Having full belief in the Shahada will give you true happiness on Earth and in Heaven.

Allah...
'Say, "Indeed, my prayer, my acts of worship, my life and my death are for Allah, Lord of the worlds"' - Quran 6:162.

Day 160
Gift a smile

What to do

Smile at all those you cross today, even if you don't feel like it. Let this be your gift, on this day, to yourself and to the world.

Why?

By smiling, you send positive energy and thoughts to yourself, and to those who see you, which will make you all feel good.

Allah...

Smiling pleases Allah. *'Do not think little of any good deed, even if it is just greeting your brother with a cheerful smile'* - Prophet Muhammad (pbuh).

Day 161
Visit the graveyard

What to do
Take a trip to the cemetery. Think about how one day you will go back to Allah.

Why?
Be happy knowing that all sadness in the world will end, and if you have been pleasing Allah in your life, then Allah and Heaven are waiting to welcome you.

Allah...
Prophet Muhammad (pbuh) told Muslims to visit cemetries as it will remind you of Allah, and that life is short, and Heaven is forever.

Day 162
Learn about the weather

What to do
Weather changes every day in your life so learn about the science behind it. How does Allah make snow? What is the purpose of rain? How is wind formed?

Why?
Learning something new and interesting will stop you from getting bored, amaze your mind and make you feel happy.

Allah....
Such learning will also show you how magnificent Allah is for creating all this. *'Do you not see that Allah makes the clouds move gently, then joins them together, then stacks them in layers?...'* - Quran 24:43.

Day 163
Ask Allah for what you want

What to do

Ask Allah for whatever you want. Do you want to have fun at school? A pet cat? Allah is the Greatest. If you ask Him for something, then He will give it to you in some way or another. Du'aa (asking Allah) is your strongest power in the world.

Why?

Be happy knowing you have this special power called 'du'aa'.

Allah...

'...indeed I am near. I answer the prayer of every caller (silent or audible) when he calls upon Me ...' - Quran 2:186. 'when He wills anything, His only command is to say "Be!" – and it is'- Quran 36:82

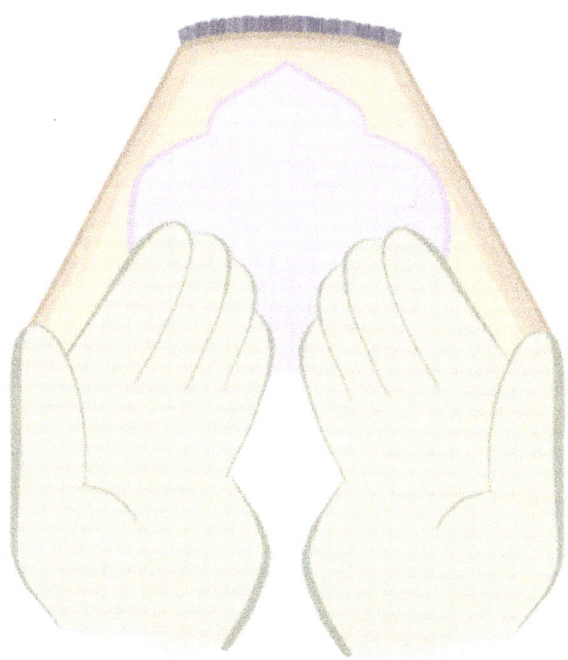

Day 164
Gaze up at the sky

What to do
Lie down outside and stare up at the sky. Watch how the clouds move but it is the Earth that's actually moving. Look out for birds. Know that the stars you see at night are still there during the day. Where is Allah's Heaven? Imagine you're sat on a cloud looking down.

Why?
Escaping from the plainness of the day will bring you joy.

Allah...
'Do they not look at the sky above them? How We have made it and beautified it, and there are no flaws in it?' - Quran 50:6.

Day 165
Be nice to 3 people

What to do

Do something nice for 3 people today. Perhaps help your aunty clean up? Play with your brother? Call up your grandfather to say hello? But don't expect things back. Do nice things because it pleases Allah and your purpose is to please Him.

Why?

Doing good things for nothing in return means you won't be disappointed by people and will be happy because Allah is happy.

Allah...

'We feed you for only Allah's pleasure. We desire no reward, nor thanks from you' - Quran 76:9.

Day 166
Notice Allah's signs

What to do

Notice everything you see, feel, hear, touch and smell all day. These are signs of Allah – your soupy egg, your wiggly fingers, the ticking clock.

Why?

Seeing Allah's signs will show you how kind, great and amazing He is. For this, you will love Him, worship Him and feel happy that He is everywhere around you.

Allah...

Allah says; *'Verily! In the creation of the Heavens and the Earth, and in the alternation of night and day, there are indeed signs for those who have intelligence'* - Quran 3:190.

Day 167
Visualise Heaven

What to do

Close your eyes for 10 minutes and imagine being in Heaven. Imagine being more beautiful than any person on Earth, floating to moons and stars, playing catch with a thousand best friends. Imagine meeting Allah. Ask Allah to give you Heaven one day, and *insha'Allah* He will.

Why?

Smile, be excited and look forward to Heaven.

Allah...

'...*There you shall have whatever your heart desires, and you shall have whatever you ask for. This is the hospitality from the Most Forgiving, the Most Merciful*' - Quran 41:31-32.

Day 168
Find ways to laugh

What to do
Do something that makes you laugh. Maybe prank your brother (keep it light), tickle your mother, watch a funny video online.

Why?
Laughter makes you feel good, relaxes your body, de-stresses you and improves your health.

Allah...
Alhamdulillah for the laughter that Allah gifts you with; *'And if you were to count the blessings of Allah, never will you be able to count them'* - Quran 14:34.

Day 169
Don't disrespect Allah

What to do

Don't complain about anything because it is disrespecting Allah. You started with nothing when you were born, and Allah has given you; lots of toys, a home, yummy food, a family, so if you still complain then Allah will not be pleased.

Why?

When you complain less and are more grateful, you will feel happier.

Allah...

Alhamdulillah for all that Allah has given: *'Then which of your Lord's favours will you deny?'* - Quran 55:13.

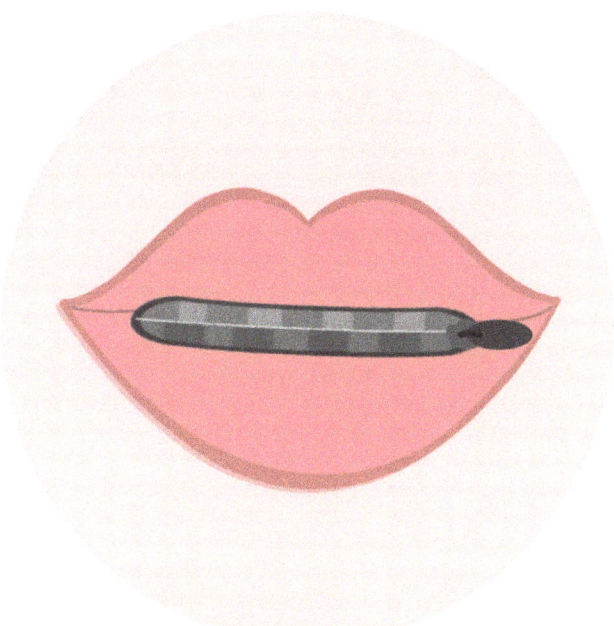

Day 170
Speak good

What to do
Speak no bad words, don't complain, don't get angry, don't shout, don't backbite.

Why?
You will notice your negative feelings disappear and more positive feelings appear, making you feel good.

Allah...
Allah will be pleased with this; *'Blessed is the person who speaks good...'* - Prophet Muhammad (pbuh).

Day 171
Go for a short walk

What to do
Go for a short walk in the daylight. Put your technology away, breathe in the fresh air and observe Allah's creations.

Why?
Walking, especially in the daylight, makes your body relax, keeps it healthy, clears your mind and boosts your happiness.

Allah...
Whilst you're out, marvel at the world Allah has created. '..."Our Lord! You did not create (all) of this without a purpose, glory be to You"...' - Quran 3:191

Day 172
Note a positive moment

What to do
Write down one positive thing that has happened to you in the last day. It might be winning a scooting race with the neighbour; how fast did you go? What does your scooter look like? Were you very happy? Read the note throughout the day.

Why?
When you write about good things, and keep reading them, your mind relives the good times and this will make you feel happy again.

Allah...
Thank Allah for this moment. He says '*...if you are grateful, I will certainly grant you more [favours]...*' - Quran 14:7.

Day 173
You are very lucky

What to do
Realise, that if you are able to obtain and read this book, then you are probably in the top 20% of the wealthy people in the world. You have spare money and an education to read. Allah could've easily put you in the bottom 80%.

Why?
When you are grateful, you are happier.

Allah...
Alhamdulillah for being one of the luckiest; *'And if you were to count the blessings of Allah, never will you be able to count them'* - Quran 14:34.

Day 174
Don't worry about the future

What to do

Don't worry about the future; your tasks for tomorrow, not having enough money, whether you'll pass your exams. Do you know what will happen tomorrow? No. Will worrying help? No. Don't worry and instead ask and trust Allah to do what is best for you.

Why?

Asking and trusting Allah will help you stop worrying and feel happier.

Allah...

'*...And whoever places his trust in Allah, Allah is Sufficient for him, for Allah will surely accomplish His Purpose...*' - Quran 65:3.

Day 175
Worries become memories

What to do
Pick a date from the last year. Remember what made you happy and sad at that time. See how Allah helped you through the sad part and you are no longer sad?

Why?
Allah will also help you with current sadness, and soon they will be forgotten too, *insha'Allah*. Know this and smile.

Allah...
Allah tells us life on Earth will be soon forgotten. *'This worldly life is a trivial [fleeting] gain. Undoubtedly, the Hereafter, is really a place to live'* - Quran 40:39.

Day 176
Sleep well

What to do
Have 8 hours sleep tonight. Turn off your gadgets, put your toys away, hug your pillow, and close your eyes.

Why?
Sleep is very important for your mind and body to feel happy and energised the next day. And it is worth more than $60,000 a year!

Allah...
Alhamdulillah for the gift of sleep. *'And remember when He made slumber fall upon you as a means of serenity from Him'* - Quran 8:11.

Day 177
Call a good friend

What to do
Meet or call a good friend. A good friend is a good person, who is positive, doesn't complain and argue, and shows happiness.

Why?
Friendship with good people is one of life's greatest joy, as their good vibes will spread to you.

Allah...
Prophet Muhammad's (pbuh) advice is that friend's vibes spread and so to keep friends *'whose appearance reminds you of God, and whose speech increases you in knowledge, and whose actions remind you of the Hereafter'*.

Day 178
Make a To-Do list

What to do
Organise yourself and make a to-do list. List what needs to be done today; homework, play, pray.

Why?
When you plan your day, you will get more things done and this will make you feel less stressed and happier.

Allah...
Before you begin, say *bismillah* (in the name of Allah) and ask Allah to help with your tasks; *'You alone do we worship and You alone do we seek for help'* - Quran 1:5.

Day 179
Do your 5 daily prayers

What to do

As a Muslim, your sole purpose in life is to worship Allah. One important way of doing this is by praying 5 times a day. So do this today. This is an act of love and devotion to Allah.

Why?

When you do your 5 prayers, you will feel like a winner as you've completed the purpose of your day.

Allah...

Allah says; *'I have not created jinn and mankind (for any purpose) except to worship Me'* - Quran 51:56.

Day 180
Drink lots of water

What to do
Carry a water bottle with you everywhere, and drink lots of water (1.5 litres). Did you know your body is made of 80% water?

Why?
When you drink enough water it boosts your energy, improves happiness, flushes out toxins, helps you think better and makes you look fresher.

Allah…
Thank Allah for this great blessing and know that He; '… *created every living thing from water*' - Quran 21:30.

Day 181
Visualise your goals

What to do

Do you have a goal at the moment; like learning to skate or wanting to pass your exams? Imagine you've done it. How does it feel? What do others say? Focus on the end. Let that excitement keep you going.

Why?

The excitement of imagining you've completed your goal will make you happy.

Allah...

Also ask Allah for help with your goal, and He will. '...*indeed I am near. I answer the prayer of every caller (silent or audible) when he calls upon Me ...*' - Quran 2:186.

Day 182
Money doesn't make you happier

What to do

It is a fact that having lots of money or things doesn't actually make you happier. Having enough money for decent food, shelter and clothing is important but once you have that, having a toy car rather than a toy speedboat doesn't make you that much happier. Your positive mind is what makes a difference.

Why?

Knowing this will make you stop wanting more, and give your heart peace.

Allah...

'Riches does not mean, having a great amount of property, but riches is self-contentment' - Prophet Muhammad (pbuh).

Day 183
Slow down

What to do

Slow down today. Don't rush your lunch, enjoy the flavours. Walk slowly, enjoy the scenery. Pray slowly, enjoy the peace. Speak slowly, enjoy the chat.

Why?

A slower day is a more peaceful day and gives you less stress and more happiness.

Allah...

Take time to appreciate all Allah has put around you; *'..."Our Lord! You did not create (all) of this without a purpose, glory be to You"...'* - Quran 3:191.

Day 184
Learn about history

What to do

Learn about the history of your country. What kind of house would you have lived in 200 years ago? What jobs would your parents have done? What shops were around? What was life like without technology? Is life much better these days?

Why?

Learning something new and interesting will stop you from getting bored, amaze your mind and make you feel happy.

Allah...

Allah will be pleased that you are learning; *'and say: 'My Lord! Increase me in knowledge'* - Quran 20:114.

Day 185
Will this please Allah?

What to do

Before you do anything, ask yourself; 'will this please Allah?' When you decide what to wear, whether to pick a flower for your mother, or whether to get angry at your brother for hiding your doll, let Allah's pleasure be the reason for your actions.

Why?

By putting Allah's pleasure first you will have a successful day, as making Allah pleased is even better than having Heaven.

Allah...

'....But the greatest bliss (happiness) is the Good Pleasure of Allah. That is the ultimate success' - Quran 9:72

Day 186
3 things you're grateful for

What to do

Write down 3 things you are grateful for. Maybe it's the water play fight you had in the garden, the chocolate chip cookie you ate or having a nice rest after a long day? Keep the list with you all day.

Why?

When you are grateful for what you have, you will be happier.

Allah...

Also, thank Allah for all these things He has given you – He will be pleased with you and give you even more. '...*If you are grateful, I will certainly grant you more [favours]...*' - Quran 14:7.

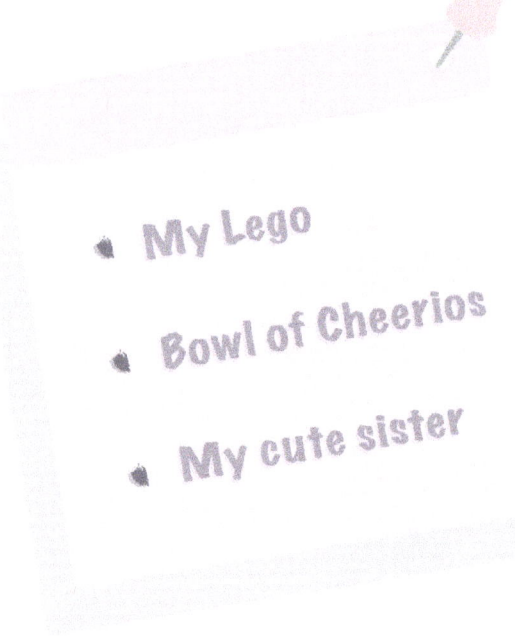

Day 187
Keep thoughts lively

What to do

Keep your thoughts lively and colourful. If you sit with a friend who moans constantly you wouldn't like it and would want to leave. Think of your thoughts like a friend talking to you. If you have an argument with your sister, don't go on about it in your mind or if you're feeling tired don't moan inside.

Why?

When your thoughts are happy, you will feel happy.

Allah...

Allah will be pleased with your happy self too; *'Blessed is the person who speaks good...'* - Prophet Muhammad (pbuh).

Day 188
Nothing in life lasts

What to do

Nothing lasts. This is the sweetness and bitterness of life. Every sadness and joy you have will not last. Your lollipop will be eaten, your bruised knee will get better, your soft skin will become wrinkly.

Why?

Knowing this will help you enjoy good moments before they fly away, and stop you from worrying about sad moments knowing they too, will fly away.

Allah...

'This worldly life is a trivial [fleeting] gain. Undoubtedly, the Hereafter, is really a place to live' - Quran 40:39.

Day 189
Live simply

What to do

Live simply. Don't eat too much, avoid designer brands, don't chase the fancy toys.

Why?

A simple life is a happier life, as you will stress less about always wanting new things and you will be able to share with the poor more.

Allah...

Allah will be pleased if you live simply and are giving; *'The son of Adam will not pass away from Allah until he is asked about five things...'*, the fourth being; *'how did he spend his wealth...'* - Prophet Muhammad (pbuh).

Day 190
Spend time with family or friends

What to do
Spend some time with your family or friends. Have a chat, play, do chores together.

Why?
Allah made you in such a way that you have a natural human need to be close with others. This brings happiness.

Allah...
This will please Allah; 'Allah will ask on the Day of Judgment: "Where are those who loved each other for the sake of My glory? Today – on a day when there is no shade but mine – I shall shade them with My shade"' - Prophet Muhammad (pbuh).

Day 191
Ask Allah for your wishes

What to do

Ask Allah for your wishes. To have good weather this weekend? A nice coat? Allah is the Giver and Taker of everything. If you ask Him for something, then He will give it to you in some way or another. Du'aa (asking Allah) is your strongest power in the world.

Why?

Be happy knowing you have this special power called 'du'aa'.

Allah...

Allah says '...indeed I am near. I answer the prayer of every caller (silent or audible) when he calls upon Me ...' - Quran 2:186. 'when He wills anything, His only command is to say "Be!" – and it is'- Quran 36:82.

Day 192
Spend time in nature

What to do
Spend at least 30 minutes outside today. Try and go to a beautiful, natural environment such as the beach, a park, the river or the woods.

Why?
Fresh air and daylight will refresh your mind and body, and make you feel happier.

Allah...
When out, look for signs of Allah; *'to Allah belong the east and the west, wherever you turn, there is the face of Allah...'* - Quran 2:115.

Day 193
Learn about dreams

What to do

You dream every single night, so find out what causes us to have good dreams and bad dreams? Why do we dream? Do they mean anything? What does science say? What does islam say?

Why?

Learning something new and interesting will stop you from getting bored, amaze your mind and make you feel happy.

Allah...

Allah will be pleased that you are learning; *'And say: My Lord increase me in knowledge'* - Quran 20:114.

Day 194
5 things in Heaven

What to do
Write down 5 things that you dream to have. Do you want; a million doughnuts? To be able to ski on water? Have a supercar? Ask Allah for it and truly believe you will have them in Heaven.

Why?
Heaven is real, and one day you will have all these things plus more! Smile and look forward to it.

Allah...
Allah says '... *In Heaven, there will be whatever the heart desires, whatever pleases the eye ....*' - Quran 43:71.

Day 195
Help someone

What to do

Help someone, solely for the love of Allah. Can you help babysit your nieces, help your mother put the dishes away after dinner, massage your father's feet?

Why?

You will feel happy that you have helped someone and made them smile.

Allah...

Allah will be pleased with this and reward you. *'Allah will ask on the Day of Judgment: "Where are those who loved each other for the sake of My glory? Today – on a day when there is no shade but mine – I shall shade them with My shade"'* - Prophet Muhammad (pbuh).

Day 196
Plan something fun

What to do

Plan something fun for this month. A picnic with your friends? A sleepover with your cousins? A baking day with your mother? Put a date into your diary.

Why?

Now you have something to look forward to and that will make you feel happy.

Allah...

Alhamdulillah for fun days; *'Then which of your Lord's favours will you deny?'* - Quran 55:13.

Day 197

Note a recent positive moment

What to do

Write down one positive thing that has happened to you in the last day. It might be that you learnt a new prayer? How long did it take? How do you feel? Read the note throughout the day.

Why?

When you write about good things, and keep reading them, your mind relives the good times and this will make you feel happy again.

Allah...

Thank Allah for this moment. He says '...*if you are grateful, I will certainly grant you more [favours]*...' - Quran 14:7.

Day 198
Magical moments

What to do

Every moment is a magical moment. When you sleep, you enter into the magic of dreams. When you wake up, the world is waiting to see how you will make it a better place. When you smile at your father, the love from your heart warms the room. When you pray, Allah turns to hear you.

Why?

Smile and enjoy the magic that takes place around you.

Allah...

Alhamdulillah for all moments; 'And if you were to count the blessings of Allah, never will you be able to count them' - Quran 14:34.

Day 199
The Greatest is always with you

What to do
If you feel sad, close your eyes, hold your heart and know that Allah, the Greatest, is always with you.

Why?
Find comfort and happiness that Allah is with you. Always.

Allah...
'Be not sad. Surely Allah is with us' - Quran 9:40. *'... remember Me. I will remember you...'* - Quran 2:152. *'...Allah is sufficient for us...'* - Quran 3:173.

Day 200
A thank you letter

What to do
Write a thank you letter to your father, aunty, friend or someone else. Thank them for, maybe the way your father listens to you talk, or how your friend always shares her crisps, or maybe how your mother fills your water bottle every night.

Why?
This person will feel happy getting this letter, and you will realise how happy you should be to have this person in your life.

Allah...
Allah will be pleased with your letter and you will be rewarded. *'He who does not thank people, does not thank Allah'* - Prophet Muhammad (pbuh).

> Dear Firdous,
>
> I just want to thank you for being my sister. I love how you play catch with me! We have...

Day 201
Make time to exercise

What to do
Take 30 minutes out to do some exercise, even if you don't feel like it. Go for a run round the block, run up and down the stairs at home or do a body workout in your bedroom.

Why?
Scientists say that exercise is very important for happiness as when you exercise, chemicals are sent to your brain that make you feel happy. Exercise also makes you healthier, look trimmer, think better and sleep well.

Allah...
Thank Allah for gifting you a healthy body to exercise; *'Then which of your Lord's favours will you deny?'* - Quran 55:13.

Day 202
Have a clear out

What to do

Get rid of clutter; things you haven't used in a year, or don't need. Pens, books, teddy bears. Give them away to charity or throw them away. Live for today and trust in Allah for tomorrow.

Why?

Having too many things will give you stress. Living simply and also giving to poor people in the world, will make you feel happy.

Allah...

Allah will be pleased too; *'...The righteous is the one who...gives wealth, in spite of love for it, to relatives, orphans, the needy...'* - Quran 2:177

Day 203
Watch life around you

What to do
Watch life around you. Perhaps on your way to school, listen to the noise of the traffic, watch children walking, notice the fluttering leaves in the trees.

Why?
Escaping from thoughts of yourself and letting your mind see the amazing things Allah surrounds you with will make you feel happy.

Allah...
Subhan'Allah for all Allah has created; *'To Allah belong the east and the west, wherever you turn, there is the face of Allah...'* - Quran 2:115.

Day 204
Your heart is a ticking timer

What to do

Feel your heart beat. Tick tock tick tock. It is like a ticking timer. The alarm has been set for when it is time for you to go back to Allah. As your heart ticks, use every second to please Allah - remember Him, pray, be nice, smile, share, be thankful, don't argue.

Why?

Be happy knowing that you will meet Allah and His Heaven.

Allah...

'The one who remembers death most often and the one who is well-prepared to meet it; these are the wise; honorable in this life and dignified in the Hereafter' - Prophet Muhammad (pbuh).

Day 205
Diarise your tasks

What to do

If you have a lot of things to do, then write them down in a diary. School homework, mosque homework, tidying your room, making a card for your brother, finishing your lego build, helping your mother in the kitchen.

Why?

Being organised will make you feel less stressed and happier.

Allah...

Ask Allah to help you with your tasks; *'You alone do we seek for help'* - Quran 1:5.

Day 206
Accept what Allah has given

What to do
Accept what Allah has decided for your life. Your intelligence, your past sadness, your pile of books. Allah is the most-wise, makes the best decisions and He knows what is good for you. So be grateful, be patient and trust Allah to be doing what is best for you.

Why?
Accepting Allah's decisions about your life will make you feel at peace.

Allah...
Accepting Allah's decision will please Him; *'Say: "nothing shall ever happen to us except what Allah has ordained for us. He is our Mawla (protector)." And in Allah let the believers put their trust'* - Quran 9:51.

Happiness Every Day *for* Kids

Day 207
Give money to the needy

What to do

Give some of your saving money to the poor of this world. Even if it's just a little, it is your intention of helping others and pleasing Allah that counts.

Why?

You will be pleased, the poor will be pleased and Allah will be pleased.

Allah...

'Do not withhold your wealth, (for if you do), Allah will withhold His blessings from you' - Prophet Muhammad (pbuh)

Day 208
Renew your life's purpose

What to do

Spend two minutes – in the morning, afternoon and evening – to stop, close your eyes, and remember your life's purpose. 'I am here to please Allah'. So act on it; be nice to others, pray, be thankful, don't complain, remember Allah.

Why?

Doing what you were born to do will make you feel happy. It will also please Allah and earn you Heaven.

Allah...

'I have not created jinn and mankind (for any purpose) except to worship Me' - Quran 51:56.

Day 209
You have more good than bad

What to do

Be happy with what you have right now, no matter how bad other things are. Even if you have no heating at home, or your parents are going through a divorce, there will still be some good things - like having a home and both your parents alive.

Why?

When you focus on good things, your mind will forget the bad things, and you will feel happier.

Allah...

Allah says; *'certainly, with every hardship there is ease'* - Quran 94:5.

Day 210
Make others happier

What to do
Today, don't dwell on your own happiness. Make people around you happier. Maybe make toast for your uncle, share your sweets with friends, help your neighbour with gardening.

Why?
When you make others happy, it will make you feel happy too.

Allah…
Also, Allah will be happy with you; '…*And do good (to others); surely Allah loves the doers of good*' - Quran 2:195.

Day 211
Life could be worse

What to do
If you are unhappy about something, think about how it could be worse. If your brother is annoying you, imagine if you had no brother. If your room is too small, imagine having no bedroom.

Why?
You should be feeling grateful now, and when you are grateful, you are happier.

Allah...
Prophet Muhammad (pbuh) said; 'look at those people who have less than you and never look at those who have more than you, this will ensure that you will not depreciate Allah's favours'. Alhamdulillah.

Day 212
Make dreams come true

What to do

What would your dream life on Earth be like? Would you be an artist? Be a great baker? Live on a farm? Write it down on a piece of paper and stick it to your wall. Start working towards your dreams now.

Why?

Having dreams and ambitions will give you new excitement and enjoyment in life.

Allah...

Before you begin, say *bismillah* and ask Allah to help; *'You alone do we worship and You alone do we seek for help'* - Quran 1:5.

Day 213
Put 10 joys in your day

What to do
Give yourself 10 joys today. Write them down. It could be; eating chocolate, drinking juice, playing with lego, reading a book, watching a cartoon, twirling your little sister round the room?

Why?
That's a lot of little joys in the day that will make you happy.

Allah...
Alhamdulillah for the little joys Allah has given you; *'And if you were to count the blessings of Allah, never will you be able to count them'* - Quran 14:34.

Day 214
Everyone has sadness

What to do

Know that everyone you see today has had or will have some sadness in their lives. Broken hearts, money troubles, lost toys, illness? Give a smile, kind word or prayer.

Why?

Think of others, rather than dwelling on your own sadness.

Allah...

'Do you think that you will enter Paradise without such [trials] as came to those who passed away before you? They were afflicted with severe poverty, ailments and were shaken, until the Prophet [pbuh] and those with him who had faith said "when will the help of Allah come?" Surely, the help of Allah is near' - Quran 2:214.

Day 215
Take your mind back

What to do

Take your mind back a year ago, and write what will happen in that year. Will you start school? Get a new brother? Lose your grandfather? Read it as though you are yet to live that year.

Why?

See how you learnt to be patient in bad times and thankful in good times? Do the same this year and you will be just fine.

Allah...

Allah will reward you for your gratitude and patience; '...*If you are grateful, I will certainly grant you more [favours]...*' - Quran 14:7; '*I have rewarded them this day for their patience...*' - Quran 23:111.

Day 216
Turn off technology

What to do
For a couple of hours, turn off all electronic devices – phone, computer, T.V. Do something of quality; play a board game with your family, have a chat with your sister, read a good book, try making something.

Why?
Electronic devices waste time, affect sleep and increase sadness.

Allah...
Thank Allah for the simple and natural gifts He has given you. *Alhamdulillah* (all praise and thanks be to Allah).

Day 217
Remember Allah

What to do

Say *Allahu akbar* (Allah is the Greatest) 100 times. Because He is the Greatest for creating the world, Heaven and you. Say *SubhanaAllah* (Glory be to Allah) 100 times. Because glory be to Him for the beauty around you. Say *Alhamdulillah* (All praise and thanks be to Allah) 100 times. Because of everything He has given you.

Why?

Doing your life's purpose of worshipping Allah will give your soul joy.

Allah...

'Surely, in the remembrance of Allah do hearts find rest' - Quran 13:28.

Day 218
Spend time with a loved one

What to do

Take some time out to spend quality time with someone you love – friend or family. Perhaps paint with your older sister? Play in the garden with your father? Read a book to your mother?

Why?

Allah made you in such a way that you have a natural human need to be close with others. So this will make you happy.

Allah...

'And Allah has made for you from your homes a place of rest' - Quran 16:80.

Day 219
Watch a travel programme

What to do

Watch a travel programme - watch something about a man's journey to India through the slums of Bombay? Or maybe about a traveller's visit to villages in Africa? Or an explorers trek in the Amazon rainforest?

Why?

There is a great world out there, so spread the wings of your mind, escape from sadness and fly into another land for a new view on life.

Allah...

Allah will be pleased as you will learn more about Him; *'say [o Muhammad]: "travel on the Earth..."'* - Quran 6:11.

Day 220
3 things you're grateful for

What to do

Write down 3 things you are grateful for. Maybe this is your English speaking school? Your swing set? Your soft rug?

Why?

When you are grateful you will be happier.

Allah...

Also, thank Allah for these things He has given – He will be pleased with you. *'Therefore remember Me. I will remember you. And be grateful to Me and do not be ungrateful'* - Quran 2:152.

Day 221
Your wishes in Heaven

What to do

Write down 5 things that you dream to have. Do you want; the fastest car in the universe? The prettiest necklace? The ability to fly? Ask Allah for it and truly believe you will have them in Heaven.

Why?

Heaven is real, and one day you will have all these things plus more! Smile and look forward to it.

Allah...

Allah says; '... *In Heaven, there will be whatever the heart desires, whatever pleases the eye ....*' - Quran 43:71.

Day 222
Go for a stroll

What to do

Go for a 30 minute stroll somewhere pleasant – along the river, in the park, by the beach? When you look at the trees, birds, sun, mountains, flowers – remind yourself that these things are in constant worship of Allah.

Why?

This will refresh your mind and body, and also inspire you to worship Allah too.

Allah...

'Do you not see that all within the Heavens and on Earth prostrate to Allah – the sun, the moon, the stars; the hills, the trees, the animals; and a great number of mankind?' - Quran 22:18.

Day 223
Ask Allah for what you want

What to do

Ask Allah for whatever you want. Do you want a holiday? Want a happy day? Allah is the Giver and Taker of everything. If you ask Him for something, then He will give it to you in some way or another. Du'aa (asking Allah) is your strongest power in the world.

Why?

Be happy knowing you have this special power called 'du'aa'.

Allah...

Making du'aa pleases Allah too; *'...indeed I am near. I answer the prayer of every caller (silent or audible) when he calls upon Me ...'* - Quran 2:186. *'when He wills anything, His only command is to say "Be!" – and it is'*- Quran 36:82.

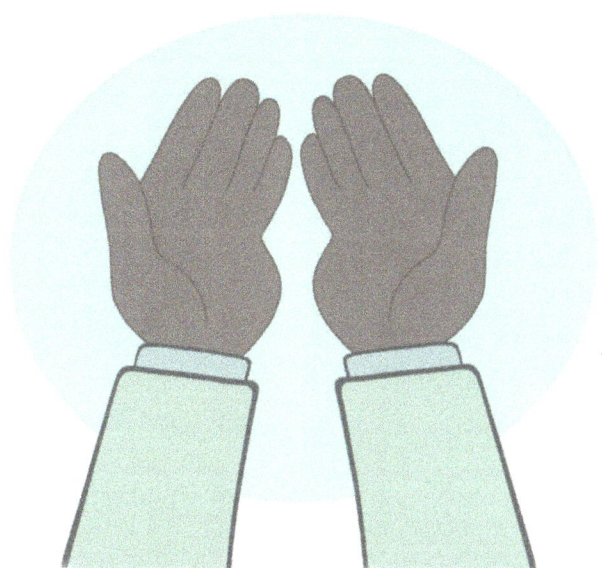

Day 224
Stop and stare

What to do
Stop and stare at everything and every moment around you.

Why?
There are marvellous things and moments around you every day - enjoy them.

Allah...
'Verily! In the creation of the Heavens and the Earth, and in the alternation of night and day, there are indeed signs for those who have intelligence' - Quran 3:190; '..."Our Lord! You did not create (all) of this without a purpose, glory be to You"...' - Quran 3:191.

Day 225
Meditate

What to do

Meditate for 10 minutes - switch off the lights, sit on the floor, with your hands on your legs, close your eyes, breathe in for 2 seconds then release. With each breath say "Allah", reminding yourself that the reason your Lord keeps you alive and breathing is so you may worship Him.

Why?

This is a perfect way to step away from your busy life and bring peace to your mind.

Allah...

'Surely, in the remembrance of Allah do hearts find rest' - Quran 13:28.

Day 226
Visit your family

What to do
Go visit family. Put your technology away and enjoy this special bonding moment. Pay attention, smile, laugh, play, talk.

Why?
Allah made you in such a way that you have a natural human need to be close with others. Spending time with family brings happiness.

Allah...
Allah will be pleased with you too; *'the best of you is the one who is best to his family'* - Prophet Muhammad (pbuh).

Day 227
Wake up early

What to do

Get up early today. The earlier you wake up, the more blessed your day will be, the less rushing around you will be doing and the more time you will have for prayers, school work, exercise, hobbies, family time.

Why?

A blessed and stress-free day is a happy day.

Allah...

Prophet Muhammad (pbuh) said; *'the early morning has been blessed for my ummah'*.

Day 228
Be patient with your sadness

What to do
With any sadness you might have, be patient. To do this, you must accept this decision Allah has made, trust Allah that it is for the best and then still please Him by doing good.

Why?
Being patient and trusting Allah when bad things happen will make you feel less sad, and open the doors of Heaven for you.

Allah…
Allah will say; 'I have rewarded them this day for their patience and faithfulness: they are indeed the ones that have achieved bliss…' - Quran 23:111.

Day 229
Do something different

What to do

Plan to go to a local event - a funfair, a market, a charity event or a festival. Or maybe arrange an outdoor get together with friends or family – a long countryside walk, a visit to the beach, or a play around in the local park.

Why?

Looking forward to the refreshing change in activity and scenery will boost your spirits.

Allah...

Alhamdulillah for being able to plan things; *'Then which of your Lord's favours will you deny?'* - Quran 55:13.

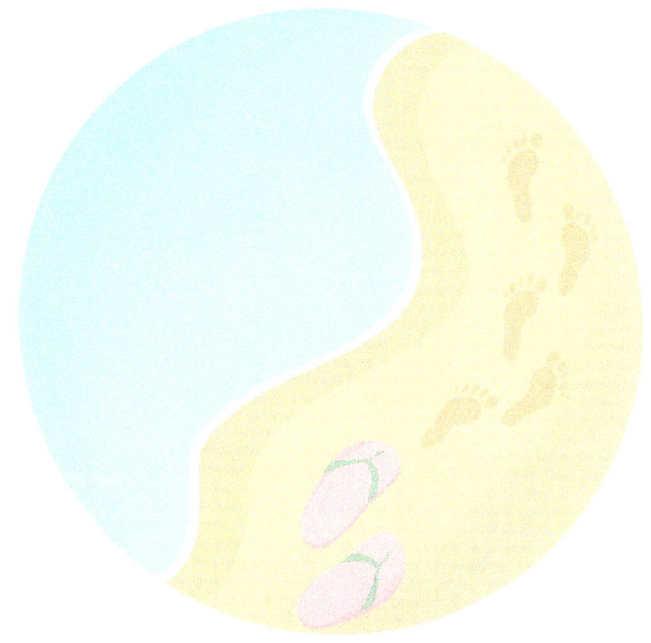

Day 230
Day of worship

What to do

When doing anything today, do it to please Allah so it becomes a day of worship. Smile at your mother, be kind to your neighbour, be thankful for your drink, pray, talk to Allah, sleep well, don't sin - Allah loves all these things.

Why?

You were born to only please and worship Allah. And so doing the things you were born to do will make you happy.

Allah...

'I have not created jinn and mankind (for any purpose) except to worship Me' - Quran 51:56.

Day 231
Look good and feel good

What to do
Wash yourself well, dress nicely and smell fresh, even if you are just staying at home.

Why?
If you look good and smell good then you will feel good.

Allah...
Also, Allah will be pleased if you are clean, neat and well-dressed. *'Allah is beautiful and likes beauty'* - Prophet Muhammad (pbuh).

Day 232
Spend money for Allah

What to do

Spend some of your savings for the pleasure of Allah. Perhaps you could buy a sandwich for a homeless man, give a few coins to the local mosque, or buy a rose for your mother.

Why?

Scientists say when you give to people, it will make you feel happier.

Allah...

Allah will be pleased and reward you many times more; *'The likeness of those who spend for Allah's sake is like a grain which grows seven ears, every single ear has a hundred grains. Allah multiplies (increases the reward of) for whom He wills...'* - Quran 2:261.

Day 233
Eat outdoors

What to do

Have breakfast, lunch or a late afternoon snack outdoors somewhere. You could go to your garden or the local park.

Why?

Fresh air and daylight will refresh your mind and body, and make you feel happier.

Allah...

Alhamdulillah for the outdoors: *'Or who has made the Earth firm to live in; made rivers in its midst; set mountains on it, and has placed a barrier between the two seas? [Can there be another] god besides Allah?...'* - Quran 27:61.

Day 234
Remember Allah

What to do
Think of Allah with every breath. Think of His power, kindness, and existence when you see the sunrise, hear tweeting birds, taste food on your tongue, use your complex tablet, feel your beating heart.

Why?
Allah is your reason to breathe, so thinking of Him will bring peace to your heart.

Allah...
'To Allah belong the east and the west, wherever you turn, there is the face of Allah...' - Quran 2: 115. *'Surely, in the remembrance of Allah do hearts find rest'* - Quran 13:28.

Day 235
Note a positive moment

What to do

Write down one positive thing that has happened to you in the last day. It might be the walk you went on with your older sister; where did you go? What did you talk about and see? Read the note throughout the day.

Why?

When you write about good things, and keep reading them, your mind relives the good times and this will make you feel happy again.

Allah...

Thank Allah for this moment. He says '...*if you are grateful, I will certainly grant you more [favours]...*' - Quran 14:7.

> My cousins Muhammad and Abu Bakr came around yesterday and we had a huge football match in the park. The best part is that my team won! And then we did a barbecue together. There were lots of positive moments but winning was the best!

Day 236
Be gentle

What to do
Be gentle; speak softly using kind words, smile often, be well-mannered, and do good deeds. If someone upsets you, still respond with gentleness.

Why?
People will love the gentle you, and you will love the gentle you, making your heart feel happy.

Allah...
'...Allah is gentle and He loves gentleness. He rewards for gentleness what is not granted for harshness and He does not reward anything else like it' – Prophet Muhammad (pbuh).

Day 237
Do some exercise

What to do

Get at least 30 minutes of exercise today. Go for a brisk walk around the block, a bike ride, or run up and down the stairs at home.

Why?

Scientists say that exercise is very important for happiness as when you exercise, chemicals are sent to your brain that make you feel happy. Exercise also makes you healthier, look trimmer, think better and sleep well.

Allah...

Thank Allah for gifting you a healthy body to exercise; *'Then which of your Lord's favours will you deny?'* - Quran 55:13.

Day 238
Be inspired by Prophet Muhammad

What to do

When you feel sad, remember the trials of Prophet Muhammad (pbuh). He was the most beloved of Allah yet was beaten, driven out of Mecca, lost his children, tied stones around his stomach when he was hungry and so on. Yet still his patience, his trust in Allah and his love for Him was unshakable. Be inspired.

Why?

You will be tested, but feel comfort knowing that Heaven is for you if you are patient and trust Allah.

Allah...

'I have rewarded them this day for their patience and faithfulness: they are indeed the ones that have achieved bliss...' - Quran 23:111.

Day 239
Post a quote

What to do

Write and post an inspirational quote into your neighbour's letterbox. It could be a verse from the Quran; *'be not sad. Surely Allah is with us'* - 9:40. Or something like; *'change your thoughts and you change your world'* - Norman V Peale.

Why?

This may brighten your neighbour's day and make you feel good about it.

Allah...

Allah will also be pleased; *'Blessed is the person who speaks good...'* - Prophet Muhammad (pbuh).

Day 240
Write 3 things you're grateful for

What to do
Write down 3 things you are grateful for. Maybe the glazed doughnut you had this morning? Being alive? Having a good friend?

Why?
When you are grateful for what you have, you will be happier.

Allah...
Also, thank Allah for all these things He has given you – He will be pleased with you. *'Therefore remember Me. I will remember you. And be grateful to Me and do not be ungrateful'* - Quran 2:152.

3 things I am grateful for today
1. My brown eyes
2. My favourite book
3. My new room

Day 241
Say yes

What to do

Say yes to something that you would usually say no to. Maybe say yes to trying carrots? Or say yes to playing car games with your cousin brother? Or playing out even if it's raining?

Why?

Trying new things will open up your experiences and may bring new enjoyment into your life.

Allah...

Also thank Allah for these new opportunities of happiness. *'Then which of your Lord's favours will you deny?'* - Quran 55:13.

Day 242
Plan a treat

What to do
Plan to treat yourself today. Perhaps by having your favourite dinner, or watching your favourite film, or having a bubble bath?

Why?
Look forward to knowing a treat is coming, and really enjoy the pleasure it brings.

Allah...
Alhamdulillah for the simplest of blessings that Allah gives you every day; *'Then which of your Lord's favours will you deny?'* - Quran 55:13.

Day 243
Learn about the internet

What to do
Find out how the internet works. How does a message you send get to your friends? How does online shopping work? How is information stored? Who made this?

Why?
Learning something new and interesting will stop you from getting bored, amaze your mind and make you feel happy.

Allah...
This is also an act of worship as Allah tells us to seek knowledge; *'and say: `My Lord! Increase me in knowledge'* - Quran 20:114.

Day 244
Talk to Allah in the night

What to do

Try to wake up for tahhajud, the pre-Fajar prayers. Sit up in the night and talk to Allah about your life, your wants, your sadnesses, your hopes. He listens the most at that time.

Why?

After talking to Allah and knowing He is listening, you will feel comforted.

Allah...

Prophet Muhammad (pbuh) said: *'our Lord descends to the lowest Heaven during the last third of the night, inquiring: "Who will call on Me so that I may respond to him? Who is asking something of Me so I may give it to him? Who is asking for My forgiveness so I may forgive him?"'*

Day 245
Reject negative thoughts

What to do

Do not allow any bad thoughts to enter your head or words to come out of your mind. No anger, no jealousy, no sulking, no sadness, no arguing, no ungratefulness, no impatience and no complaining. Think about the good things like your new skateboard or your funny brother.

Why?

If you think about good things only you will feel happier.

Allah...

'Blessed is the man who speaks good and is triumphant; or keeps silent in the face of evil and is secure' - Prophet Muhammad (pbuh).

Day 246
Get rid of extras

What to do
Try to live simply. Check your room to see what you don't need and can give away or throw away; books, pencils, old clothes?

Why?
A simple life is a happier life, as you will stress less about always wanting new things and you will be able to share with the poor more.

Allah...
Think of the Prophet (pbuh) and what little he lived with. *'Whoever has extra provision should give from it to the one who has no provision...'* - Prophet Muhammad (pbuh).

Day 247
Start learning

What to do
Think of one thing you have always wanted to learn and start today. Have you always wanted to learn arabic? Learn some words online. Have you always wanted to learn how to sew? Borrow a sewing kit.

Why?
New challenges will give you new types of happiness in life.

Allah...
Allah will be pleased as He tells us to seek knowledge; *'and say: "My Lord! Increase me in knowledge'* - Quran 20:114.

Day 248
Raise money for charity

What to do
Pick a charity and make a plan today to help raise money for them. Maybe you could organise a group walk around the local park and get sponsorships? Or maybe you could sell cupcakes to your friends and family?

Why?
Spending your time helping others will make them happy, you happy and will take your mind off sad things.

Allah...
Also, Allah will be pleased. '...*And do good (to others); surely Allah loves the doers of good*' - Quran 2:195.

Day 249
Be happy with what you have

What to do

Be happy with what you have in life. The length of your hair, your trainers, the size of your family. Allah is the most-wise, makes the best decisions and He knows what is good for you. So be grateful for what you have, be patient with what you don't have, and trust Allah to be doing what is best for you.

Why?

Accepting Allah's decisions about your life will make you happier.

Allah...

'O Allah, make me content with what you have provided me, send blessings for me therein, and place for me every absent thing with something better' - Prophet Muhammad.

Day 250
Go get some ice cream

What to do

Go get some ice cream with your friends or family. Enjoy a new flavour and a chat with your companions.

Why?

This is a random and simple way to boost your mood.

Allah...

Alhamdulillah for ice cream and companionship. 'And if you were to count the blessings of Allah, never will you be able to count them' - Quran 14:34.

Day 251
Hard times are a blessing

What to do

If you are feeling down, wondering why God, the most Kind, is giving you sadness, then realise that this sadness is a good thing. Allah knows that it is when you are at your saddest that you are most likely to turn to Him for help. And when you turn to Him for help, He is pleased. When He is pleased, He will give you Heaven.

Why?

Knowing that your sadness is actually a ticket to enter Heaven, will make you feel better.

Allah..

'...He will give you [something] better than what was taken from you...'
- Quran 8:70.

Day 252
Explore a new place

What to do
Find a new natural surrounding; maybe a beach, park or walking route, and explore it.

Why?
Exploring a new part of Allah's Earth will give you a fresh source of happiness.

Allah...
Allah will be pleased as He tells us to travel and appreciate His beauties; *'say [O Muhammad]: "travel on the Earth..."'* - Quran 6:11.

Day 253
Write 'B' for Bismillah

What to do

Write a 'B' on the back of your hand. 'B' for *bismillah* (in the name of Allah). Every time you see the B, say *bismillah* before every activity you begin; waking up, going to school, starting lunch.

Why?

Saying *bismillah* will bring Allah's blessing into your tasks and remind you of your purpose. Your heart will feel peace.

Allah...

Allah will be pleased that everything you are doing is in His name; *'I have not created jinn and mankind (for any purpose) except to worship Me'* - Quran 51:56.

Day 254
Share 3 good things

What to do

Share with someone 3 good things that happen today. Keep an eye out for them. It may be that funny joke your brother tells you, that delicious slice of pie you eat or the sticker you get from your teacher.

Why?

Spotting the good things in your day will make you smile.

Allah…

And thank Allah; *'So take what I have given you and be of the grateful ones'* - Quran 7:144.

Day 255
Lift people's mood

What to do

Show positivity to everyone. Be the one that brings a smile to people's faces because you are cheerful, full of good words and give good vibes. Don't be the one who brings other's moods down because you always complain and are grumpy.

Why?

By being positive you will feel good, and make others feel good.

Allah...

Allah will be pleased with your positivity; *'to smile in the face of your brother is charity given on your behalf'* - Prophet Muhammad.

Day 256
Make decisions quickly

What to do

Make today's minor daily decisions quickly. Your life will not change if you wear green socks instead of blue, or whether to have an apple or an orange. Ask Allah to choose what's best for you, make a decision, trust Him and don't look back.

Why?

Don't worry about small decisions, trust Allah and you will be happier.

Allah...

'Say: "Nothing shall ever happen to us except what Allah has ordained for us. He is our Mawla (protector)." And in Allah let the believers put their trust' - Quran 9:51.

Day 257

Note a positive moment

What to do

Write down one positive thing that has happened to you in the last day. It might be that you built a castle with lego; how long did it take? Did you enjoy building it? What colour is it? Read the note throughout the day.

Why?

When you write about good things, and keep reading them, your mind relives the good times and this will make you feel happy again.

Allah...

Thank Allah for this moment. He says '...*if you are grateful, I will certainly grant you more [favours]...*' - Quran 14:7.

Day 258
Accept Allah's decisions

What to do

Accept all that Allah has decided for you. Whether you are tall or short. Whether you have a mother or not. Allah is the most-wise, makes the best decisions and He knows what is good for you. So be grateful, be patient and trust Allah to be doing what is best for you.

Why?

Accepting Allah's decisions about your life will make you feel happy.

Allah...

This will also please Allah. '*...And it may be that you dislike a thing which is good for you and that you like a thing which is bad for you. Allah knows but you do not know*' - Quran 2:216.

Day 259
Look at the night sky

What to do

Tonight, grab a blanket, go outside, lay down and look at the stars, the moon and, possibly, the planets – Mercury, Mars, Venus, Jupiter and Saturn. Count the stars, work out how far they are, what it must be like in space and how great Allah is to have created billions of stars, planets, moons.

Why?

This is a simple, beautiful and magical moment that will give you joy.

Allah...

SubhanAllah; '..."Our Lord! You did not create (all) of this without a purpose, glory be to You"...' - Quran 3:191.

Day 260
3 things you're grateful for

What to do
Write down 3 things you are grateful for. Maybe the fact that you haven't fallen for quite a while? Or that it's a day off school so you can rest and play? Or maybe the ice lolly you had?

Why?
When you are grateful you are happier.

Allah...
Also, thank Allah for all these things He has given you – He will be pleased and give you even more. *'...If you are grateful, I will certainly grant you more [favours]...'* - Quran 14:7.

I am grateful for...

1. My blue water bottle

2. The sunshine

3. Sunday

Day 261
Try fasting

What to do
Try fasting today. Maybe don't eat so much and just drink water.

Why?
Fasting cleans your soul and body, reminds you of the good that you have been given in life, helps you think of the poor and makes you feel grateful, and so, happier.

Allah...
Alhamdulillah for plenty of food. *'And if you were to count the blessings of Allah, never will you be able to count them'* - Quran 14:34.

Day 262
Think of Allah the most

What to do
Think of and love Allah the most, more than friends, family or yourself.

Why?
Allah is the Greatest and is for forever. He created you, gives you everything, is always there for you, and will take you to Heaven. Loving Him the most and thinking about Him the most will give your heart peace.

Allah...
'Surely, in the remembrance of Allah do hearts find rest' - Quran 13:28. '...But those that truly believe, love Allah more than anything else...' - Quran 2:165.

Day 263
Be inspired by others

What to do
What would you like to be one day? Maybe an artist, or a storyteller? If so, look into some famous artists or storytellers that you'd want to be like.

Why?
Watching successful people will motivate you to become like them one day, and give you something to look forward to.

Allah...
Ask Allah to help you reach your dreams – He can and He will, insha'Allah; *'You alone do we worship and You alone do we seek for help'* - Quran 1:5.

Day 264
Meditate

What to do
Spend 10 minutes in the morning, afternoon and evening meditating. Sit in a quiet corner, with your eyes closed, focussing on your breathing. Say 'Allah' with each breath, reminding yourself that the reason that Allah keeps you alive and breathing is so that you may worship Him.

Why?
This is a perfect way to step away from your busy life and bring peace to your mind.

Allah...
'Surely, in the remembrance of Allah do hearts find rest' - Quran 13:28.

Day 265
Ask Allah for what you want

What to do

Ask Allah for what you want. Maybe you want to be a top footballer? Allah is the Giver and Taker of everything. If you ask Him for something, then He will give it to you in some way. Du'aa (asking Allah) is your strongest power in the world.

Why?

Be happy knowing you have this special power called 'du'aa'.

Allah...

Making du'aa pleases Allah too; *'...indeed I am near. I answer the prayer of every caller (silent or audible) when he calls upon Me ...'* - Quran 2:186. *'when He wills anything, His only command is to say "Be!" – and it is'* - Quran 36:82.

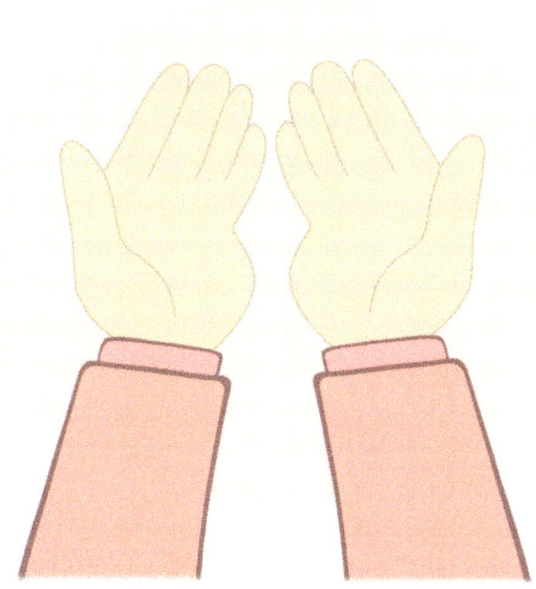

Day 266
Take photos of 3 things

What to do

Take a photo of 3 things that make you happy. It could be your home, your city, your prayer mat, your book collection. Print the photos and put them on your wall.

Why?

Seeing the things you love often, will make you smile often.

Allah...

Thank Allah whenever you see the photos; *'Then which of your Lord's favours will you deny?'* - Quran 55:13.

Day 267
Notice Allah's signs in the day

What to do
Notice everything you see, feel, hear, touch and smell all day. These are signs of Allah – the taste of toothpaste, the meowing cat next door, the sound of the rain.

Why?
Seeing Allah's signs will show you how kind, great and amazing He is. For this, you will love Him, worship Him and feel happy that He is everywhere around you.

Allah...
Allah says; *'Verily! In the creation of the Heavens and the Earth, and in the alternation of night and day, there are indeed signs for those who have intelligence'* - Quran 3:190.

Day 268
Life is not forever

What to do

If you are feeling sad, remind yourself that nothing in this life lasts, which includes your sadness. So be patient, ask Allah to do what is best for you and say 'I trust you Allah'.

Why?

Knowing all sad things will one day end, and you will meet Allah and His Heaven will make you feel good.

Allah...

'Oh mankind, indeed you are ever toiling towards your Lord, painfully toiling... But you shall meet Him' - Quran 84:6.

Day 269
Believe in Heaven

What to do

Write down 5 things that you dream to have. Do you want; a conversation with Allah? Forever happiness? To meet your great grandma? Ask Allah for it and truly believe you will have them in Heaven.

Why?

Heaven is real, and one day you will have all these things plus more! Smile and look forward to it.

Allah...

Allah says; '... *In Heaven, there will be whatever the heart desires, whatever pleases the eye ....*' - Quran 43:71.

Day 270
Get some exercise

What to do
Exercise today even if it's just for 30 minutes. Go for a brisk walk round the block, a run in the park, or 100 skips on your rope.

Why?
Scientists say that exercise is very important for happiness as when you exercise, chemicals are sent to your brain that make you feel happy. Exercise also makes you healthier, look trimmer, think better and sleep well.

Allah...
Prophet Muhammad (pbuh) advises you to look after your body, which is a gift from Allah. *'Then which of your Lord's favours will you deny?'* - Quran 55:13.

Day 271
Eat moderately

What to do
When eating, don't fill your stomach to the top.

Why?
Eating too much can make you feel sick, sleepy, lazy, put on weight and is also, not Islamic.

Allah...
Prophet Muhammad (pbuh) said: 'Nothing is worse than a person who fills his stomach. It should be enough for the son of Adam to have a few bites to satisfy his hunger. If he wishes more, it should be: one-third for his food, one-third for his liquids, and one-third for his breath'.

Day 272
You are perfect

What to do

You are perfect – think about this. Don't look at anyone but yourself. Think about how; your eyes allow you to see the beauty of life; your teeth are tough to chew on candy, your fingers allow you to write, your soul feels love, your mind puts thoughts into action and you are the best compared to insects and animals.

Why?

You are a walking, talking, smiling miracle. Greater than anything man has ever invented. Smile.

Allah...

Alhamdulillah for your body; *'We have indeed created humankind in the best of molds'* - Quran 95:4.

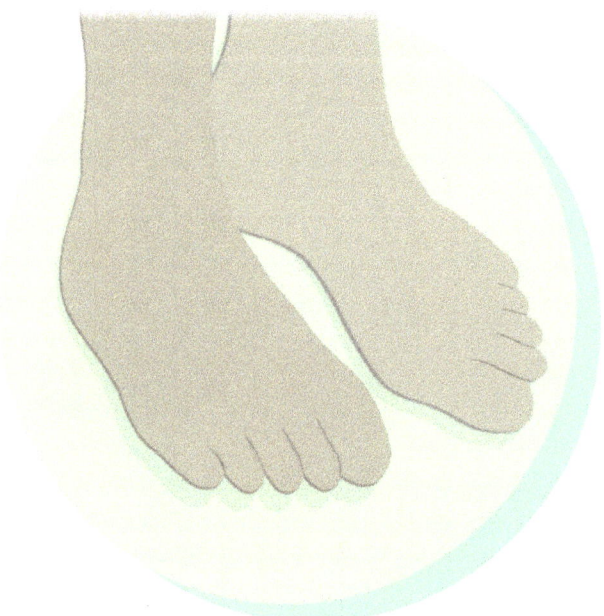

Day 273
Turn hardships into blessings

What to do
Turn the sad things into something good. Think of the things that you are unhappy about. Now don't complain, but raise your hands and ask Allah to do what is best for you in this. Say 'I trust you Allah'. Then be patient, trust Allah and love Him.

Why?
If you are patient, Allah will reward you with Heaven. There, you've turned your sadness into something good. Smile.

Allah...
'Peace be upon you, because you persevered in patience! Excellent indeed is the final home (Paradise)!' - Quran 13:24.

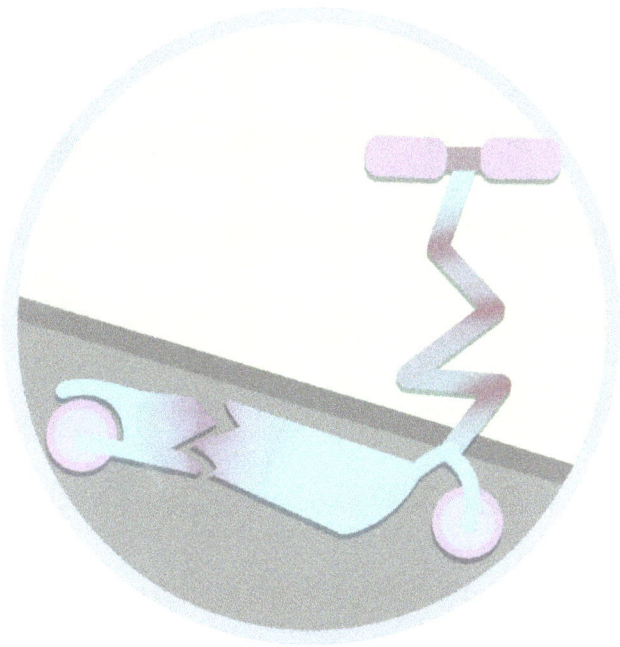

Day 274
Invite someone for dinner

What to do
With permission, invite someone round to share your dinner tonight. Treat your guest well and make them feel special.

Why?
Your heart will feel happy in the company of your guest and seeing them smile, and you won't have time to think of any worries.

Allah...
Allah will be pleased with your good deed; '...*And do good (to others); surely Allah loves the doers of good*' - Quran 2:195.

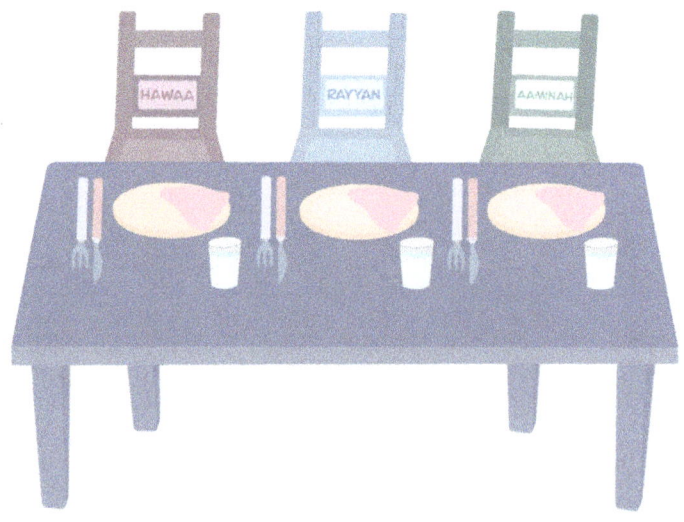

Day 275
Think, speak and do positive

What to do
In the morning, go to the mirror, look at yourself and say 'today, I promise to think, speak and do only good things. And I promise to block any bad thoughts, words and actions'. Keep that promise.

Why?
You will notice your negative feelings disappear and more positive feelings appear, making you feel good.

Allah...
Allah will be pleased with this; *'Blessed is the person who speaks good...'* - Prophet Muhammad (pbuh).

> Today I promise to think, speak and do only positive things.

Day 276
Act how you want to feel

What to do
If you want to feel happy today, perhaps at school, then first you must act happy. Be positive, joke with your friends, smile at the teachers, run around in the playground.

Why?
When you act happy, real feelings of happiness will soon follow.

Allah...
Ask Allah to make you feel happy too; *'Call upon Me; I will respond to you'* - Quran 40:60

Day 277
Look up at the sky

What to do
Often today, look up at the sky. Imagine being taken away with the clouds to see the wonders of the world. Imagine what is beyond the sky and know that the promised Heaven is somewhere out there.

Why?
Escape from the little things in life and let the sky's wonders fill you with joy.

Allah...
Heaven Allah says; *'In a lofty Paradise, where they shall neither hear harmful speech nor falsehood. Therein will be a running spring. Therein will be thrones raised high, and cups set at hand. And cushions set in rows, and rich carpets (all) spread out'* - Quran 88:10-16.

Day 278
Note a positive moment

What to do

Write down one positive thing that has happened to you in the last day. It might be that your baby cousin came round; how cute is he? Did he giggle with you? What did you play? Read the note throughout the day.

Why?

When you write about good things, and keep reading them, your mind relives the good times and this will make you feel happy again.

Allah...

Thank Allah for this moment. He says *'...if you are grateful, I will certainly grant you more [favours]...'* - Quran 14:7.

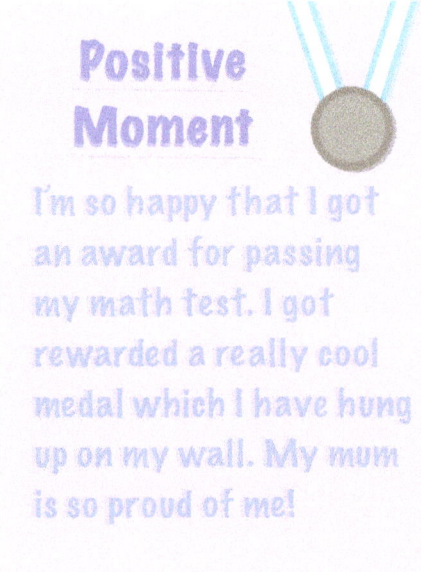

Positive Moment

I'm so happy that I got an award for passing my math test. I got rewarded a really cool medal which I have hung up on my wall. My mum is so proud of me!

Day 279
Drink plenty of water

What to do
Carry a water bottle with you everywhere, and drink lots of water (1.5 litres). Did you know your body is made of 80% water?

Why?
When you drink enough water it boosts your energy, improves happiness, flushes out toxins, helps you think better and makes you look fresher.

Allah...
Thank Allah for this great blessing and know that He; *'... created every living thing from water'* - Quran 21:30.

Day 280
Thank you letter to Allah

What to do

Write a gratitude letter to Allah. Thank Allah for all the blessings He has given you. Explain how you love your tablet or how thankful you are for your parents. There will be so many things to write about!

Why?

Writing this letter will show you how much you have to be happy about.

Allah...

This will please Allah; *'And if you were to count the blessings of Allah, never will you be able to count them'* - Quran 14:34.. *'...And Allah will soon reward the grateful ones'* - Quran 3: 144.

Day 281
Clear out a box

What to do
Pick a box in your room and have a clear out. Get rid of clutter, things you haven't used in a year, or don't need. Colouring pens, lego, shoes – give them away to charity or throw them away. Live for today and trust in Allah for tomorrow.

Why?
Having too many things will give you stress. Living simply and also giving to poor people in the world, will make you feel happy.

Allah...
Giving to charity pleases Allah; *'Whoever has extra provision should give from it to the one who has no provision'* - Prophet Muhammad (pbuh).

Day 282
Smile all day

What to do
Smile lots today, even if you don't feel like smiling.

Why?
When you smile, positive signals and thoughts are sent to your brain that then make you feel happy. Smiling at other people will also make them happy.

Allah...
Smiling pleases Allah too and will gain you reward; *'Do not think little of any good deed, even if it is just greeting your brother with a cheerful smile'*- Prophet Muhammad (pbuh)

Day 283
Keep your mind calm

What to do
Keep your mind calm no matter what is happening around you - even if it's windy outside, you've dropped your ice cream or fallen out with your friend. Think happy thoughts, take away sad thoughts and remember that life is about pleasing Allah.

Why?
Life on the outside can't always be controlled by you, but if you keep your mind inside positive then you will feel happy.

Allah...
Remember your purpose, as Allah says; *'I have not created jinn and mankind (for any purpose) except to worship Me'* - Quran 51:56.

Day 284
Life is a journey to Allah

What to do

As you carry out your daily tasks today, remember that life is a journey from Allah to Allah. Nothing else. You came from Allah and will return to Him. Spend your day as though you are actually on your way back to Allah; please Him, do good things, and keep remembering Him.

Why?

When you remember this you won't feel sad about the little worries and will look forward to the day you will return to the Greatest.

Allah...

'Surely, to Allah we belong, and to Him we shall return' - Quran 2:156.

Day 285
Help someone

What to do

Help someone today. Give some of your toys to a charity shop? Make a sandwich for your mother? Teach your little sister how to count?

Why?

You will feel happy that you have helped someone and made them smile.

Allah...

Allah will be pleased with this and reward you. '*...And do good (to others); surely Allah loves the doers of good*' - Quran 2:195.

Day 286

Go to a museum or castle

What to do

Plan a trip to a museum soon. Or if you can't go, take your mind back to hundreds of years ago. Imagine – working in a British coal mine for 12 hours a day, making a fire with sticks for dinner in India, or even walking alongside Prophet Muhammad (pbuh) in Arabia as his companion.

Why?

This will fascinate you and also make you feel happy to live in modern times.

Allah...

SubhanAllah for the different lives Allah has created; *'Travel through the Earth and observe how Allah began creation. And then Allah will produce the final creation'* - Quran 29:20.

Day 287
Sleep well

What to do
Have 8 hours sleep tonight. Turn off your gadgets, put your toys away, hug your pillow, and close your eyes.

Why?
Sleep is very important for your mind and body to feel happy and energised the next day. And it is worth more than $60,000 a year!

Allah...
Alhamdulillah for the gift of sleep. *'It is Allah who has made the night for you to rest...'* - Quran 40:61.

Day 288
Go out into nature

What to do
Go out somewhere nice today, like the park, beach or the countryside. Run, walk, skip. Breathe in the fresh air, feel the wind on your face, and hear the birds sing.

Why?
Fresh air and daylight will refresh your mind and body, and make you feel happier.

Allah...
When out look at all the things Allah has made and say wow, subhan'Allah. '...And they think deeply about the creation of the Heavens and the Earth, [saying] "Our Lord! You did not create (all) of this without a purpose, glory be to You"...' - Quran 3:191.

Day 289
Slow down

What to do

Slow down today. Don't rush your dessert, enjoy the flavours. Walk slowly, enjoy the scenery. Pray slowly, enjoy the peace. Speak slowly, enjoy the chat.

Why?

A slower day is a more peaceful day and gives you less stress and more happiness.

Allah...

Take time to appreciate all Allah has put around you; '..."*Our Lord! You did not create (all) of this without a purpose, glory be to You*"...' - Quran 3:191.

Day 290
Donate to charity

What to do
Contact 10 of your family and friends today and ask them to donate unused toys, clothes and toiletries for you to give to the local women's refuge or something similar.

Why?
This kindness will naturally make the recipients happy, make the ones that donated happy and make you happy.

Allah...
This pleases Allah, who will reward you; *'Whoever does good equal to the weight of an atom (or a small ant), shall see it'* - Quran 99:7.

Day 291
Thank people

What to do
When someone does something for you, thank them by saying; *'jazakAllahu khayrun'* (may Allah reward you with good). Be it if someone gives you a sweet, helps you carry your books, compliments you.

Why?
By thanking people with a prayer, they will feel happy and so will you.

Allah...
Prophet Muhammad (pbuh) said; *'whoever has a favour done for him and says to the one who did it, "jazakAllahu khayrun" has done enough to thank him'*. *'He who does not thank people, does not thank Allah'*.

Day 292
Be thankful for modern times

What to do
Be thankful for the modern times you live in. If you can have hot showers, eat a variety of world foods, use a computer, read varied books, microwave food then you are living better than a king or queen had done 400 years ago. They did not have this. Spot all the luxuries you have which were not around in the past.

Why?
This will make you feel thankful and happy.

Allah...
Alhamdulillah for modern times; *'Then which of your Lord's favours will you deny?'* - Quran 55:13.

Day 293
Everything is a loaned gift

What to do

Everything you have in your life is not yours, but is a loaned gift from Allah. Your shiny wall mirror, your toy motorbike, your feet, your bags of sweets; all of it is a loaned gift from Allah and is not yours to keep forever. Each gift will one day be taken back by Allah.

Why?

Knowing everything is borrowed will make you thankful, and help you make the most of what you have with happiness.

Allah...

'Surely, to Allah we belong, and to Him we shall return' - Quran 2:156.

Day 294
Imagine being in Heaven

What to do

Think about your final place, Heaven. Close your eyes and imagine being in Heaven. Imagine being the strongest boy ever, having a house on top of the clouds or seeing Allah. What else would you wish for? Ask Allah to take you to Heaven one day, and *insha'Allah* He will.

Why?

Smile, be excited and look forward to Heaven.

Allah...

Prophet Muhammad (pbuh) said; *'Allah says: "I have prepared for My righteous slaves that which no eye has seen, no ear has heard and it has never crossed the mind of man"'.*

Day 295
Note 3 things you're grateful for

What to do
Write down 3 things you are grateful for. Maybe the fact that you are well and healthy? Or that it's sports day at school? Or maybe your mother made your favourite dish?

Why?
When you are grateful you will be happier.

Allah...
Also, thank Allah for all these things He has given you – He will be pleased with you and give you even more. '...*If you are grateful, I will certainly grant you more [favours]...*' - Quran 14:7.

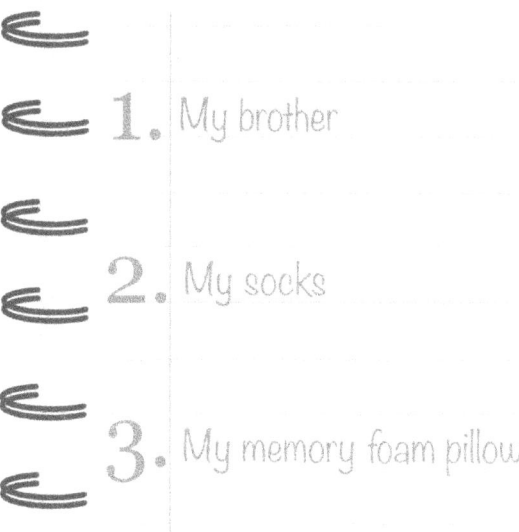

1. My brother
2. My socks
3. My memory foam pillow

Day 296
Be happy with life

What to do

Be happy about life purely because Allah wanted things to be this way. Maybe you're unhappy that you don't have the latest gadget, or that you have no brothers. But Allah, the Greatest, the most-wise, decided this for you and He makes the best decisions. So trust Him, be patient, love Him, and be happy.

Why?

Being happy with all the good and bad in life will mean... You are happy!

Allah...

Allah will love your patience and gratitude; *'peace be upon you, because you persevered in patience! Excellent indeed is the final home (Paradise)!'* - Quran 13:24.

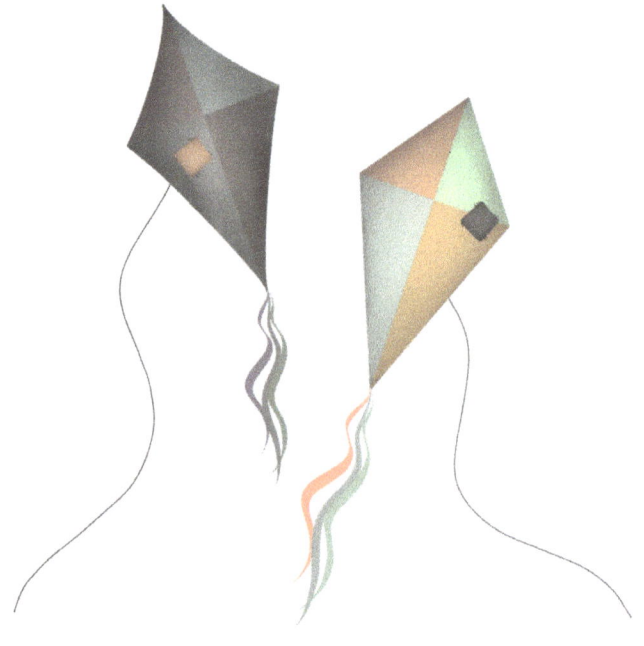

Day 297

Note a positive moment

What to do

Write down one positive thing that has happened to you in the last day. It might be the giraffe you made from playdough. What colour was it? How did you make it? Where is it now? Read the note throughout the day.

Why?

When you write about good things, and keep reading them, your mind relives the good times and this will make you feel happy again.

Allah…

Thank Allah for this moment. He says '...*if you are grateful, I will certainly grant you more [favours]*...' - Quran 14:7.

Day 298
Be amazed by plant life

What to do
Watch a documentary on plant life. Plants may seem very still but just like people and animals, plants live and die, fight amongst each other, compete for mates, reproduce, travel, but the drama is a lot slower.

Why?
Learning something new and interesting will stop you from getting bored, amaze your mind and make you feel happy.

Allah...
Did you know that even plants are in constant worship of Allah? *'...Behold, verily in these things there are signs for those who understand!'* - Quran 13:4.

Day 299
Fun times of the past

What to do

Find some photos of when you were younger. Chat about the fun times you had with your family or friends. Relive the moments when you were 1 year old or 5 years old; the time you rode your first bike or went on your first holiday abroad.

Why?

Enjoy looking back at good times and smile.

Allah...

Thank Allah for giving you these moments of happiness that maybe you never had the chance to thank Him for. *'And if you were to count the blessings of Allah, never will you be able to count them'* - Quran 14:34.

Day 300
Focus in your prayers

What to do
Fully concentrate in your prayers. When you begin, forget what is happening in the world, as you are about to have a private meeting with Allah. Give your heart, soul and body to only Allah, out of love for Him.

Why?
For your soul, this is true joy and happiness.

Allah...
'Surely, in the remembrance of Allah do hearts find rest' - Quran 13:28.

Day 301
Have a relaxed breakfast

What to do
Relax over breakfast. Eat something healthy and energy boosting – cereal, fruit, brown toast, a smoothie. Put technology away, and enjoy looking out the window.

Why?
Having a relaxing and fuel-filled breakfast will set a great start to your day, *insha'Allah*.

Allah...
Alhamdulillah for relaxing moments; *'Then which of your Lord's favours will you deny?'* - Quran 55:13.

Day 302
Accept Allah's decisions

What to do

Accept all that Allah has decided. Whether you've got lots of toys or not. Whether you have nice hair or not. Allah is the most-wise, makes the best decisions and He knows what is good for you. So be grateful, be patient and trust Allah to be doing what is best for you.

Why?

Accepting Allah's decisions about your life will make you feel at peace.

Allah...

This will also please Allah. *'...And it may be that you dislike a thing which is good for you and that you like a thing which is bad for you. Allah knows but you do not know'* - Quran 2:216.

Day 303
Note your achievements

What to do
Write a list of all your achievements. This could include an award you won at school, your sporting medals, raising money for charity, learning to ride a bike well.

Why?
You are accomplished and have done well. Feel happy.

Allah...
Alhamdulillah for your achievements; *'And if you were to count the blessings of Allah, never will you be able to count them'* - Quran 14:34.

Day 304
Life leads to Allah and Heaven

What to do

Life can be difficult when dealing with disappointment, illness, death of loved ones, or day to day unhappiness. Allah understands this and tells us to stay patient and you will finally meet Him and Heaven.

Why?

Knowing that struggles will one day end, and you will meet Allah and His Heaven will make you feel good.

Allah...

'Oh mankind, indeed you are ever toiling towards your Lord, painfully toiling... But you shall meet Him' - Quran 84:6.

Day 305
Help someone

What to do
Help someone today. Perhaps do some shopping for your neighbour, pick some flowers for your mother or say something nice to your friend.

Why?
You will feel happy that you have helped someone and made them smile.

Allah...
Allah will be pleased with this and reward you. '*...And do good (to others); surely Allah loves the doers of good*' - Quran 2:195.

Day 306
Go outdoors

What to do

Go outdoors for half an hour. Wind, rain or shine. Try and go to a natural environment; the sea, park, riverside, canal or woods.

Why?

Fresh air and daylight will refresh your mind and body, and make you feel happier.

Allah...

Notice the amazing world Allah has created; *'Or who has made the Earth firm to live in; made rivers in its midst; set mountains on it, and has placed a barrier between the two seas? [Can there be another] god besides Allah?...'*- Quran 27:61.

Day 307
Meaning of surah al-Fatiha

What to do
Learn the meaning of *surah al-Fatiha*, chapter 1 of the Quran. It is a surah that you will recite often in your life.

Why?
These are the direct words of Allah and you will feel closer to Him when you understand His book. And when you feel close to Allah, your heart is happier.

Allah...
'Surely, in the remembrance of Allah do hearts find rest' - Quran 13:28.

Day 308
Do 1 thing that makes you happy

What to do
Do one thing today that makes you happy. It may be; playing a video game, drawing, gardening, eating dry cereal or reading your favourite book.

Why?
This will make you feel happy!

Allah...
Thank Allah for this small moment of pleasure, and you will be rewarded with more *'...If you are grateful, I will certainly grant you more [favours]...'* - Quran 14:7.

Day 309
Learn about how birds fly

What to do

Learn about how birds fly. How do their wings work? What keeps them up in the air? What do they see? What happens if it's dark or windy? Do planes work the same way?

Why?

Learning something new and interesting will stop you from getting bored, amaze your mind and make you feel happy.

Allah....

Allah will be pleased that you're learning and thinking about His magnificence; *'And say: My Lord increase me in knowledge'* - Quran 20:114.

Day 310
Master your mind

What to do

Be the master of your mind, by only allowing positive thoughts into it. If you are feeling tired, focus on the time you will be able to go to bed. If you are struggling to make friends, focus on the fact that you have a nice family at home.

Why?

When you control your thoughts to think of the positive only, then you will feel much happier.

Allah...

'Certainly, with every hardship there is ease' - Quran 94:5.

Day 311

Imagine you can now see

What to do

When you wake up, imagine you have been blind for all your life. Keep that thought in your head. Open your eyes. You can see. Be amazed at everything as though you are seeing things for the first time. Look at the colour of your hands, the sky above, the flying birds, other people old and young - their actions.

Why?

You can see, many cannot. Be grateful and happy for your eyesight.

Allah...

Thank Allah for this wonderful gift of eyes; *'So take what I have given you and be of the grateful ones'* - Quran 7:144.

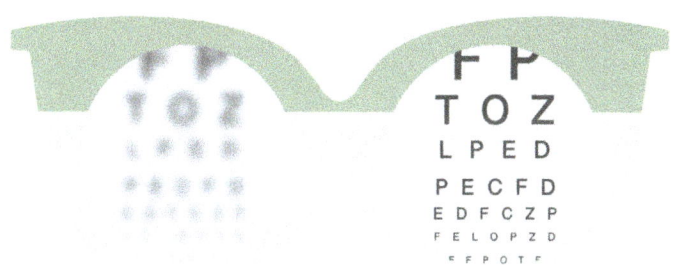

Day 312
Pick a gratitude pebble or shell

What to do
Go to the beach or a park today, and pick up a shell or a pebble that will fit in your pocket. This will be your gratitude reminder. Every time you now see this, think of something you are thankful for in that moment.

Why?
Reminding yourself of things to be thankful for will make you smile and be happy.

Allah...
Alhamdulillah; 'So take what I have given you and be of the grateful ones' - Quran 7:144.

Day 313
Ask Allah for what you want

What to do

Don't worry about things but instead ask Allah for whatever you want. Do you want to pass a test? Allah is the Giver and Taker of everything. If you ask Him for something, then He will give it to you in some way or another. Du'aa (asking Allah) is your strongest power in the world.

Why?

Be happy knowing you have this special power called 'du'aa'.

Allah...

...indeed I am near. I answer the prayer of every caller (silent or audible) when he calls upon Me ...' - Quran 2:186. *'when He wills anything, His only command is to say "Be!" – and it is'* - Quran 36:82

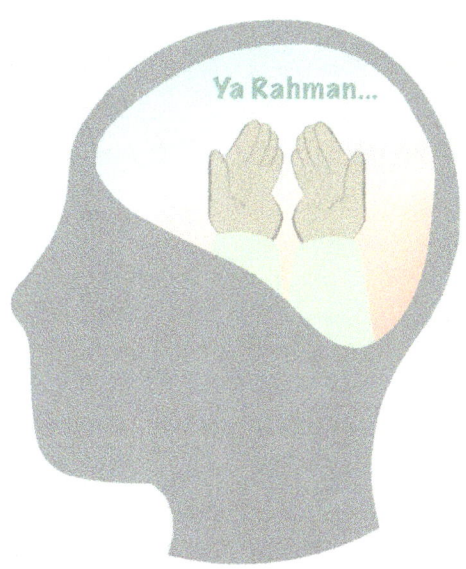

Day 314
Note 3 things you're grateful for

What to do
Write down 3 things you are grateful for. Maybe you are thankful for the grip on your trainers, the light in your room, or maybe being able to read stories well?

Why?
When you are grateful you will be happier.

Allah...
Also, thank Allah for all these things He has given you – He will be pleased with you and give you even more. '...*If you are grateful, I will certainly grant you more [favours]...*' - Quran 14:7.

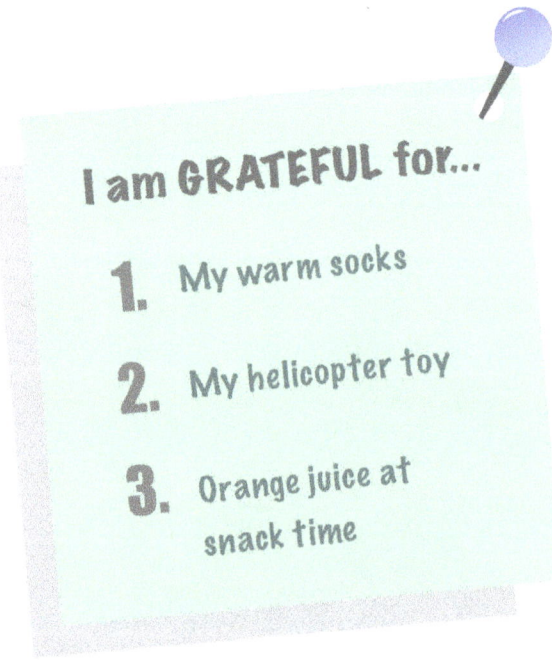

I am GRATEFUL for...
1. My warm socks
2. My helicopter toy
3. Orange juice at snack time

Day 315
Plan your day

What to do

Plan your day. Write down the things you will be doing today; go to school, do your homework, tidy your crafts drawer, pray, exercise, read a book, help your parents. Tick the list off as you go along.

Why?

When you plan your day, you will get more things done and this will make you feel less stressed and happier.

Allah...

Before you begin, say *bismillah* and ask Allah to help with your tasks; *'You alone do we worship and You alone do we seek for help'* - Quran 1:5.

Day 316
Do good for Heaven

What to do
Do you want Heaven? Where there is endless happiness and whatever you wish for? If so, then work for it, by doing things that please Allah; prayers, gratitude, patience, being nice to others, giving to charity, not lying, cheating or shouting.

Why?
Look forward to the day when you will enter Heaven and smile.

Allah...
'So give good news, to those who have faith and do good acts, that for them shall be gardens beneath which rivers flow...' - Quran 2:25.

Day 317
Put Allah at the front

What to do

Put Allah at the front of your mind. Your purpose in life is to worship, please and love Allah. Try and think about Him all the time; See the shining sun? Praise Allah. Feel a stomach ache coming on? Ask Allah to make it better. Enjoying a sandwich? Thank Allah. Having a hard time at school? Tell Allah you trust Him.

Why?

Bringing Allah into your everyday will make you happy.

Allah...

'I have not created jinn and mankind (for any purpose) except to worship Me' - Quran 51:56. 'Surely, in the remembrance of Allah do hearts find rest'- Quran 13:28.

Day 318
Your wealth has been set

What to do
Don't worry about money, and having expensive things. Allah set the amount of wealth you will get in your life, before you were born. Nothing you do will change it. But ask Allah to put blessings in what you have, so even a little can go a long way.

Why?
So stop worrying about and chasing money and expensive things, and you'll feel happier.

Allah...
Prophet muhammad (pbuh) said *'If the son of Adam ran away from his provision as he runs away from death, then his provision would find him just as death finds him.'*

Day 319
Exercise for a boost

What to do
Boost your mind and body by exercising. Go for a jog round your back yard, do 50 star jumps, or 100 skips.

Why?
Scientists say that exercise is very important for happiness, as happy chemicals are released after exercise into your brain. Also, people who exercise are healthier, look trimmer, think more clearly and sleep better.

Allah...
Prophet Muhammad (pbuh) advises you to look after your body by exercising. *'Then which of your Lord's favours will you deny?'* - Quran 55:13.

Day 320
Hang out with good people

What to do

Surround yourself with good and happy people. People who pray, are kind and positive. Try to stay away from people who are mean, swear, badly behaved and negative.

Why?

If you are around bad people their bad vibes will spread to you. But if you are around good happy people, their good happy vibes will spread to you.

Allah...

Prophet Muhammad's (pbuh) said choose friends; *'whose appearance reminds you of God, and whose speech increases you in knowledge, and whose actions remind you of the Hereafter'.*

Happiness Every Day *for Kids*

Day 321
Better yourself

What to do

Do something that will help you become a better person; read a book, learn how to draw, help your mother clean up, follow an origami video.

Why?

This will stop you from feeling bored and help you become a better person.

Allah...

Allah will be pleased that you are bettering yourself; *'and say: "My Lord! Increase me in knowledge"'*- Quran, 20:114 *'"...and do good (to others); surely Allah loves the doers of good"'* - Quran 2:195.

Day 322
Believe Allah decides the best

What to do

Whether you are going through a tough time at school or are sick, remember that this is Allah's decision – Allah is the most-wise, makes the best decisions and He knows what is good for you. So be grateful, be patient and trust Allah to be doing what is best for you.

Why?

Believing Allah's decisions are the best decisions will make you feel happy.

Allah...

'...And it may be that you dislike a thing which is good for you and that you like a thing which is bad for you. Allah knows but you do not know' - Quran 2:216.

Day 323
Kick a ball

What to do
Go kick a ball in the park or your backyard for a little while. Rain, wind or shine.

Why?
Natural daylight and exercise clear your mind, boost your energy and make you feel happier. Kicking a ball is fun too!

Allah...
Alhamdulillah; 'And if you were to count the blessings of Allah, never will you be able to count them' - Quran 14:34.

Day 324

Note a positive moment

What to do

Write down one positive thing that has happened to you in the last day. It might be the rollercoaster ride you went on; how fast was it? Did you scream at first then laugh afterwards? Read the note throughout the day.

Why?

When you write about good things, and keep reading them, your mind relives the good times and this will make you feel happy again.

Allah...

Thank Allah for this moment. He says *'...if you are grateful, I will certainly grant you more [favours]...'* - Quran 14:7.

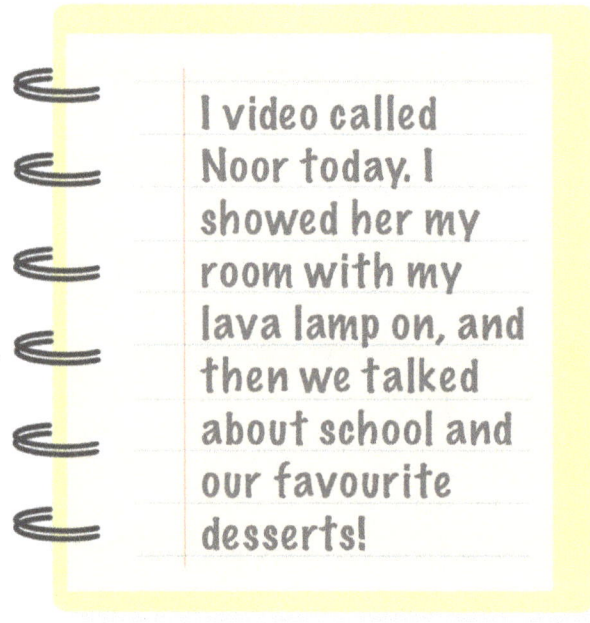

Day 325
Carry prayer beads

What to do
Carry a tasbee (prayer beads) with you everywhere today. In the car, at home, when walking. Use it to simply remember Allah. Say *Allahu akbar* (Allah is the Greatest), *Subhana'Allah* (glory be to Allah) or *Alhamdulillah* (all praise and thanks be to Allah).

Why?
Thinking of, remembering and worshipping Allah is true joy for your soul.

Allah...
'Surely, in the remembrance of Allah do hearts find rest' - Quran 13:28.

Day 326
Imagine you're not alive

What to do

Imagine you're no longer alive. Death happens to everyone, it is nothing to be scared of but a reality. So live today doing what Allah put you on Earth for; worshipping and pleasing Him.

Why?

Imagining this means that you will worry less, argue less, love more, smile more, and do more good; earning your place in Heaven

Allah...

'The one who remembers death most often and the one who is well-prepared to meet it; these are the wise; honorable in this life and dignified in the Hereafter' - Prophet Muhammad (pbuh).

Day 327
Start saving money

What to do
Save some money, even if it is a little, every week. You could earn that money by doing extra jobs for your family or neighbours.

Why?
Having money saved gives you comfort for if you need it in an emergency or would like to treat yourself.

Allah...
Ask Allah to put blessings and barakah into your savings; *'call upon Me; I will respond to you'* - Quran 40:60.

Day 328
3 things you're grateful for

What to do

Write down 3 things you are grateful for. Maybe you are thankful that your father brings money into the house? Or that your cousin took you to the beach recently? Or for your shiny hair?

Why?

When you are grateful you will be happier.

Allah...

Also, thank Allah for all these things He has given you – He will be pleased with you and give you even more. '...*If you are grateful, I will certainly grant you more [favours]*...' - Quran 14:7.

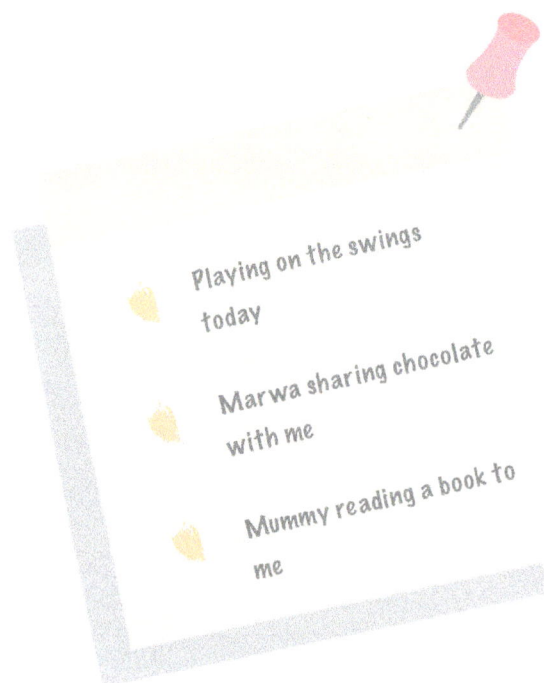

Playing on the swings today

Marwa sharing chocolate with me

Mummy reading a book to me

Day 329
Have an islamic gathering

What to do
In the evening, gather your family around and read out a hadith (report of the life of Prophet Muhammad (pbuh)).

Why?
When you gather like this, the light of faith and peace enters your heart, angels join and pile to the sky to seek your forgiveness by Allah, and bad things in your house disappear.

Allah...
Allah will be pleased with this; *'and say: My Lord increase me in knowledge'* - Quran 20:114.

Day 330
Gift the world with du'aa

What to do

Give the gift of du'aa to the world. Take 10 minutes out, raise your hands and ask Allah for the happiness of the world. Mention your family, friends and neighbours. Think of the hungry, the sad, the orphans, the sick.

Why?

Your prayers can help the world and can also help you, as everytime you make du'aa for someone else, an angel says *"Ameen! May it be for you, too"*. Feel happy.

Allah...

'Du'aa is the most potent weapon of a believer, it can change fate while no action of ours ever can' - Prophet Muhammad (pbuh).

Day 331
Be clean at all times

What to do
Be clean at all times. Shower in the morning, brush your teeth, wear clean clothes, and wash every time you go to the bathroom.

Why?
You will find being fresh and clean pleasing and re-energising.

Allah...
Allah will be pleased; *'Truly, Allah loves those who turn to Him in repentance and loves those who purify themselves'* - Quran 2:222.

Day 332
Snack outdoors

What to do

Have a snack outdoors somewhere. Go to your garden, the local park or the lakeside and eat a bag of crisps or a tub of fruit.

Why?

Fresh air and daylight will refresh your mind and body, and make you feel happier.

Allah...

Also reflect on the Earth that Allah has gifted you with. 'Or who has made the Earth firm to live in; made rivers in its midst; set mountains on it, and has placed a barrier between the two seas? [Can there be another] god besides Allah?...' - Quran 27:61.

Day 333
What do you want in Heaven?

What to do

Write down 5 things that you dream to have. Do you want; to run as fast as a Cheetah? Be as beautiful as a mermaid? Live in a palace made out of sweets? Ask Allah for it and truly believe you will have them in Heaven.

Why?

Heaven is real, and one day you will have all these things plus more! Smile and look forward to it.

Allah...

Allah says '... *In Heaven, there will be whatever the heart desires, whatever pleases the eye ....*' - Quran 43:71.

Day 334
Write an 'A' for Alhamdulillah

What to do

Write an 'A' on the back of your hand. 'A' for *Alhamdulillah* (all praise and thanks be to Allah). Every time you see that A, look around you for something that Allah has gifted you with; a good night's sleep, a tasty cheese string? Each time, smile and say *alhamdulillah*.

Why?

When you are grateful for what you have, you will be happier.

Allah...

Allah will be very pleased with you. '*...And Allah will soon reward the grateful ones*' - Quran 3:144.

Day 335

Note a positive moment

What to do

Write down one positive thing that has happened to you in the last day. It could be the big bear hug your father gave you. How did it feel, did you feel safe? Did you laugh? Read the note throughout the day.

Why?

When you write about good things, and keep reading them, your mind relives the good times and this will make you feel happy again.

Allah...

Thank Allah for this moment. He says '...*if you are grateful, I will certainly grant you more [favours]...*' - Quran 14:7.

Positive Moment

It was so much fun having a race with Firdous! I ran as fast as I could an thought I would win but she was faster and won. She was so happy and that made me feel really happy too!

Day 336
Look at your successful past

What to do

Look back at your successes of the last years. Write them down. Did you pass your exams? Raise money for charity? Make a new friend? Did you learn how to swim?

Why?

Look how blessed you have been. Well done! Imagine what successes the next 5 years could hold? Look forward to it.

Allah...

Alhamdulillah for your successes; *'And if you were to count the blessings of Allah, never will you be able to count them'* - Quran 14:34.

Day 337
Clear out a box

What to do
Pick a box and have a clear out. Books, cars, dolls. Give them away to charity or throw them away. Don't feel that you might need it one day, live for today and trust in Allah for tomorrow.

Why?
Having too many things will give you stress. Living simply and also giving to the poor, will make you feel happy.

Allah...
Allah will be pleased; *'...The righteous is the one who...gives wealth, in spite of love for it, to relatives, orphans, the needy...'* - Quran 2:177.

Day 338
Make people happy

What to do

Make people happy by being kind. Say something nice to your mother, make your brother a sandwich, open the door for a stranger, greet someone with the Islamic greeting; *assalamu'alaikum warahmatullahi wabarakatuh* (may the peace, mercy, and blessings of Allah be with you)

Why?

When you do nice things for people, they will feel happy and you will feel happy.

Allah...

Also, Allah will be happy with you; *'Is there any reward for good, other than good?'* - Quran 55:60.

Day 339
Hard times are good

What to do

If you are feeling down, wondering why 'bad things happen to good people', realise that 'bad' things do not happen to good people. Allah knows that it is when you are at your saddest that you are most likely to turn to Him for help. And when you turn to Him for help, He is pleased. And when He is pleased, He will give you Heaven.

Why?

Knowing that your sadness is actually a ticket to enter Heaven, will make you feel better.

Allah...

'...*But give good news to those who patiently persevere...*' - Quran 2:155.

Day 340
Set a new goal

What to do

Set a goal for yourself that you would want to achieve in the next year. Perhaps it is to learn how to make a cardboard doll house, play in a football team, write a story, learn to skip 2000 times? Start working on it today.

Why?

Having a new goal will give you new excitement and enjoyment in life.

Allah...

Before you begin, say *bismillah* (in the name of Allah) and ask Allah to help; *'You alone do we worship and You alone do we seek for help'* - Quran 1:5.

Day 341
Get some exercise in

What to do
Do some exercise today. Ride your scooter outside, jump on a trampoline, roller skate.

Why?
Scientists say that exercise is very important for happiness as when you exercise, chemicals are sent to your brain that make you feel happy. Exercise also makes you healthier, look trimmer, think better and sleep well.

Allah...
Thank Allah for gifting you a healthy body to exercise; *'Then which of your Lord's favours will you deny?'* - Quran 55:13.

Starjumps!

Day 342
Accept Allah's choice

What to do

Accept what Allah has chosen for you. Whether you won an award at school or not. Whether you got the last piece of cake or not. Allah is the most-wise, makes the best decisions and He knows what is good for you. So be grateful, be patient and trust Allah to be doing what is best.

Why?

Accepting Allah's decisions about your life will make you feel at peace.

Allah...

'Say: "Nothing shall ever happen to us except what Allah has ordained for us. He is our Mawla (protector)"And in Allah let the believers put their trust' - Quran 9:51.

Day 343
Revolve your day around Allah

What to do
Make your day revolve around Allah, by doing your tasks for His pleasure. When you hold your little sister's hand or study hard at school, do it because Allah is pleased.

Why?
Pleasing Allah is the purpose of your life, and so doing your life's purpose will give your heart peace and happiness.

Allah...
'Say, "Indeed, my prayer, my acts of worship, my life and my death are for Allah, Lord of the worlds"' - Quran 6:162.

Day 344
Zoom in on good things

What to do
Zoom in on the good things in your life right now; your caring grandmother, your able hands, your lego set. Zoom out of and don't think about any bad things in your life.

Why?
When you focus on good things, your mind will forget the bad things, and you will feel happier.

Allah...
Allah says; *'certainly, with every hardship there is ease'* - Quran 94:5.

Day 345
Smile all day

What to do
Smile lots today, even if you don't feel like smiling.

Why?
When you smile, positive signals and thoughts are sent to your brain that then make you feel happy. Smiling at other people will also make them feel good.

Allah...
Smiling pleases Allah too and will gain you reward; *'to smile in the face of your brother is charity given on your behalf'* - Prophet Muhammad (pbuh).

Day 346
Notice the big world

What to do
Notice the big world around you. Be amazed by the sky, the interesting behaviours of your friends, the squirrels playing in trees, the twinkle in your eye when you smile, the bright red of an apple.

Why?
When you stop thinking about the little issues and look around you instead, you will feel happier.

Allah...
SubhanAllah; '...And they think deeply about the creation of the Heavens and the Earth, [saying] "Our Lord! You did not create (all) of this without a purpose, glory be to You"...' - Quran 3:191.

Day 347
Have a treat

What to do
Find a not-so-exciting task you have for today and replace it with treat-time. Have you got tidying up to do? Homework that can wait till tomorrow? Instead do something you love - read, play a game, kick a ball, colouring.

Why?
Smile and really enjoy the pleasure your treat brings.

Allah...
Alhamdulillah for the simplest of treats that Allah gives you every day; *'Then which of your Lord's favours will you deny?'* - Quran 55:13.

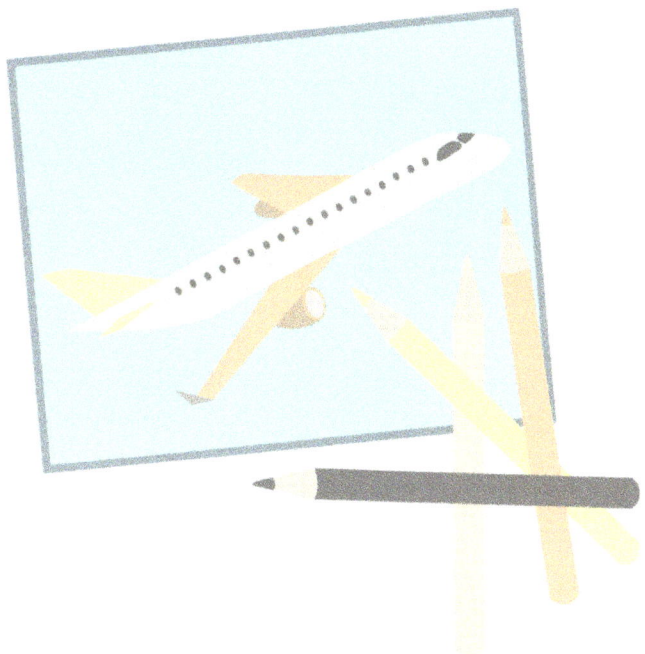

Day 348
Sleep well

What to do

Have 8 hours sleep tonight. Turn off your gadgets, put your toys away, hug your pillow, and close your eyes.

Why?

Sleep is very important for your mind and body to feel happy and energised the next day. And it is worth more than $60,000 a year!

Allah...

Alhamdulillah for the gift of sleep. *'And remember when He made slumber fall upon you as a means of serenity from Him'* - Quran 8:11.

Day 349
Sacrifice a buy

What to do

Are you saving up to buy yourself something? Sacrifice it and give the money to a charity where other children in the world do not have clean water, shoes or a school to go to.

Why?

Imagining the smile of a child's face when they can buy bread or a book with your money, will make you smile too.

Allah...

Allah will be pleased. *'...The righteous is the one who...gives wealth, in spite of love for it, to relatives, orphans, the needy...'* - Quran 2:177.

Day 350
Enjoy everything

What to do
Enjoy everything you touch, see, hear and taste - your mother's laughter, the blossomed tree outside your house, the sweet peach you bite into, the rain on your face, the soft pillow you rest your cheek on.

Why?
Savouring and enjoying all moments will make you feel happier.

Allah...
Alhamdulillah for the little things; *'And if you were to count the blessings of Allah, never will you be able to count them'* - Quran 14:34.

Day 351
Think and speak positive

What to do
Promise to think and speak only positively. If it is too cold, don't complain; think that it could be colder. When you are hungry, be glad that you'll be eating soon. When you get angry at your brother, think of his good points.

Why?
If you act negatively, you will feel more sad, but if you act and speak positively then you will feel happier.

Allah...
'Blessed is the man who speaks good and is triumphant; or keeps silent in the face of evil and is secure' - Prophet Muhammad (pbuh).

Day 352
Walk in the fresh air

What to do
Go for a short walk in the daylight. Put your technology away, breathe in the fresh air and observe Allah's creations.

Why?
Walking, especially in the daylight, relaxes your body, clears your mind and gives you a happiness boost.

Allah...
As you walk, be amazed by the world Allah has created for you; '..."Our Lord! You did not create (all) of this without a purpose, glory be to You"...' - Quran 3:191.

Day 353
Focus on your life's purpose

What to do

Your purpose in life is to worship Allah. Eat, so you have energy to please Allah, study so you can soon earn money to live your purpose, sleep so you have enough rest to worship Him, hang with family so you can show kindness which Allah loves, go out in nature so you can glorify Allah. Everything is there for you to do your purpose.

Why?

You were born to please Allah, and so nothing can make you happier than doing what you were born to do.

Allah...

'I have not created jinn and mankind (for any purpose) except to worship Me' - Quran 51:56.

Day 354
3 things you like about you

What to do

Look in the mirror and pick out 3 things that you like about the way you look. Perhaps it's the twinkle in your eyes, your white smile, your dimple? Focus on those each time you look in the mirror, smile and ignore anything you may dislike.

Why?

Focusing on your good things and being grateful will make you happier.

Allah...

Alhamdulillah – thank Allah for your small beauties. *'So take what I have given you and be of the grateful ones'* - Quran 7:144.

Day 355
You are the luckiest

What to do
Realise that you are one of the luckiest on Earth. There are 3+ billion people living worldwide on $2 a day, and it was worse hundreds of years ago for most of the world. Allah could have very easily put you in one of the poorer parts, and still can. Be grateful.

Why?
When you are grateful, you are happier.

Allah...
Alhamdulillah for being one of the luckiest; *'And if you were to count the blessings of Allah, never will you be able to count them'* - Quran 14:34.

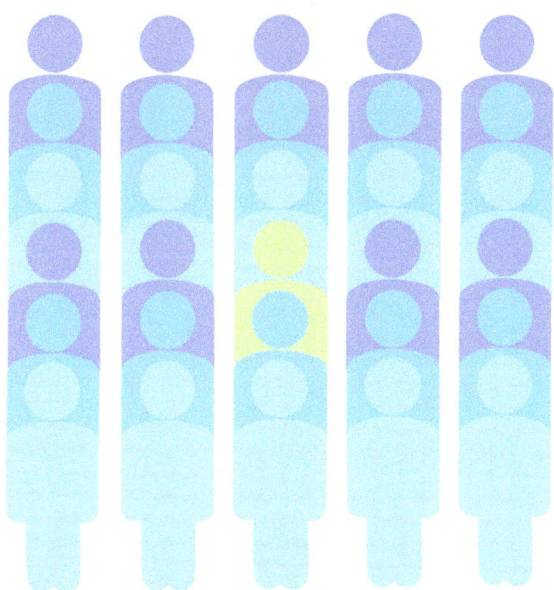

Day 356
Think of Allah the most

What to do

Think of and love Allah the most, more than your friends, family, things or yourself.

Why?

Allah is the Greatest and is for forever. He created you, gives you everything, is always there for you, and will take you to Heaven. Loving Him the most and thinking about Him the most will give your heart peace.

Allah...

'...But those that truly believe, love Allah more than anything else...' - Quran 2:165.

Day 357
Read a poem

What to do
Read a poem. Search online for spiritual poems relating to God, such as Rumi's 'A Moment of Happiness'. Or you could try other types of poems by other poets.

Why?
Words are great and reading a poem can bring joy to a different part of your mind.

Allah...
Allah tells us to seek knowledge; *'and say: "My Lord! Increase me in knowledge"'* - Quran 20:114.

Day 358
Clean your mind before sleep

What to do

As you rest your head on your pillow tonight, make effort to get rid all negative thoughts. Forgive or apologise to the person you may have argued with. Block out any worries. Sleep with Allah's name, and promise to please Him tomorrow. Think of the happiness you will have in Heaven and smile.

Why?

Sleeping with nice thoughts will make you happy and refresh you in the morning.

Allah...

'They will not hear therein ill or sinful speech. But only the saying of: Peace! Peace!' - Quran 56:25-26.

Day 359
Learn about insects

What to do
Learn about insects. Do they have a pulse? Do they breathe oxygen? What do they eat? Do they have feelings and thoughts?

Why?
Learning something new and interesting will stop you from getting bored, amaze your mind and make you feel happy.

Allah...
Did you know that every creature worships Allah? *'Do you not see that all within the Heavens and on Earth prostrate to Allah — the sun, the moon, the stars; the hills, the trees, the animals; and a great number of mankind?'* - Quran 22:18.

Day 360
Notice Allah's signs in the day

What to do

Notice everything you see, feel, hear, touch and smell all day. These are signs of Allah – the warmth of your gloves, the pencil on your paper as you write, the voice of your teacher.

Why?

Seeing Allah's signs will show you how kind, great and amazing He is. For this, you will love Him, worship Him and feel happy that He is everywhere around you.

Allah...

Allah says; *'Verily! In the creation of the Heavens and the Earth, and in the alternation of night and day, there are indeed signs for those who have intelligence'* - Quran 3:190.

Day 361
Note a recent positive moment

What to do

Write down one positive thing that has happened to you in the last day. It might be that you learnt how to make cheese pasta; what did you put in? Did it taste delicious? Who else ate it? Read the note throughout the day.

Why?

When you write about good things, and keep reading them, your mind relives the good times and this will make you feel happy again.

Allah...

Thank Allah for this moment. He says '*...if you are grateful, I will certainly grant you more [favours]...*' - Quran 14:7.

Day 362
Live like it's your last day

What to do

Live today as though it's your last day. That doesn't mean you should be sad, but to do things that you have been put on earth for - to please Allah. So do things that please Allah; go to school and learn, be kind, say your prayers, be thankful for food, make du'aa for what you want, trust Allah.

Why?

If it is your last day, then you will not have wasted it. This will make you feel happy.

Allah...

And you will have done your best in pleasing Allah, and earning a place in Heaven, *insha'Allah*.

Day 363
Write 3 things you're grateful for

What to do
Write down 3 things you are grateful for. Maybe the fact that you have a father that is kind to you? Or being able to see ladybirds in the garden? Or for the chocolate cereal you ate earlier?

Why?
When you are grateful you will be happier.

Allah...
Also, thank Allah for all these things He has given you – He will be pleased with you and give you even more. '*...If you are grateful, I will certainly grant you more [favours]...*' - Quran 14:7.

Day 364
Ask Allah for good in your life

What to do

Ask Allah for good changes in your life. Do you want a happy future? Allah is the Giver and Taker of everything. If you ask Him for something, then He will give it to you in some way or another. Du'aa (asking Allah) is your strongest power in the world.

Why?

Be happy knowing you have this special power called 'du'aa'.

Allah...

Making du'aa pleases Allah too. *'When He wills anything, His only command is to say "Be!" – and it is'*- Quran 36:82

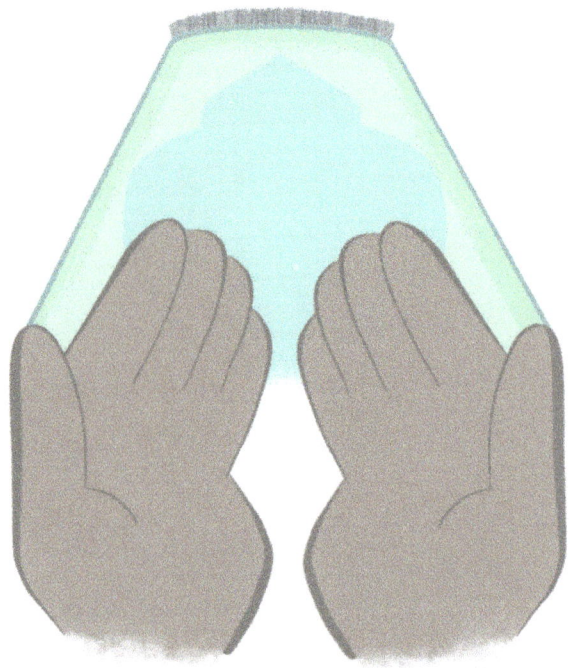

Day 365
Imagine Heaven

What to do

Think about your final place, Heaven. Imagine waterfalls of smarties, skating on an ice rink made of juice, jumping on a trampoline that takes you to the stars. What else would you wish for? Ask Allah to give you Heaven one day, and *insha'Allah* he will.

Why?

Smile, be excited and look forward to Heaven.

Allah...

Prophet Muhammad (pbuh) said; 'Allah says: "I have prepared for My righteous slaves that which no eye has seen, no ear has heard and it has never crossed the mind of man"'.

Well Done! Start again from Day 1

www.ingramcontent.com/pod-product-compliance
Lightning Source LLC
Chambersburg PA
CBHW050925240426
43668CB00021B/2430